# rapid chess improvement

**Michael de la Maza**

EVERYMAN CHESS

Everyman Publishers plc  www.everymanbooks.com

First published in 2002 by Everyman Publishers plc, formerly Cadogan Books plc, Gloucester Mansions, 140A Shaftesbury Avenue, London WC2H 8HD

Reprinted 2002

**British Library Cataloguing-in-Publication Data**
A catalogue record for this book is available from the British Library.

ISBN 1 85744 269 5

Distributed in North America by The Globe Pequot Press, P.O Box 480, 246 Goose Lane, Guilford, CT 06437-0480.

All other sales enquiries should be directed to Everyman Chess, Gloucester Mansions, 140A Shaftesbury Avenue, London WC2H 8HD
tel: 020 7539 7600 fax: 020 7379 4060
email: chess@everymanbooks.com
website: www.everymanbooks.com



EVERYMAN CHESS SERIES (formerly Cadogan Chess)
Chief advisor: Garry Kasparov
Commissioning editor: Byron Jacobs

Typeset and edited by First Rank Publishing, Brighton.
Production by Book Production Services.
Printed and bound in Great Britain by The Cromwell Press Ltd., Trowbridge, Wiltshire.

# Everyman Chess

**Books for players serious about improving their game:**

| | | |
|---|---|---|
| 1 85744 226 1 | Starting Out in Chess | Byron Jacobs |
| 1 85744 231 8 | Tips for Young Players | Matthew Sadler |
| 1 85744 236 9 | Improve Your Opening Play | Chris Ward |
| 1 85744 241 5 | Improve Your Middlegame Play | Andrew Kinsman |
| 1 85744 246 6 | Improve Your Endgame Play | Glenn Flear |
| 1 85744 223 7 | Mastering the Opening | Byron Jacobs |
| 1 85744 228 8 | Mastering the Middlegame | Angus Dunnington |
| 1 85744 233 4 | Mastering the Endgame | Glenn Flear |
| 1 85744 238 5 | Simple Chess | John Emms |

**Books for the more advanced player:**

| | | |
|---|---|---|
| 1 85744 233 4 | Attacking with 1 e4 | John Emms |
| 1 85744 233 4 | Attacking with 1 d4 | Angus Dunnington |
| 1 85744 219 9 | Meeting 1 e4 | Alexander Raetsky |
| 1 85744 224 5 | Meeting 1 d4 | Aagaard and Lund |
| 1 85744 273 3 | Excelling at Chess | Jacob Aagaard |

**Popular puzzle books:**

| | | |
|---|---|---|
| 1 85744 273 3 | Multiple Choice Chess | Graeme Buckley |
| 1 85744 296 2 | It's Your Move | Chris Ward |
| 1 85744 278 4 | It's Your Move (Improvers) | Chris Ward |

# Contents

# Ackowledgments

Special thanks to Stacy Angle, Neil Cousin, FM John Curdo, Mark Donlan, Larry Eldridge, Mark Fins, Howard Goldowski, Franklin Herman, Alan Hodge, FM Igor Foygel, NM Dan Heisman, Mark Kaprielian, NM Spencer Lower, Robert Oresick, Matthew Phelps, Harvey Reed, NM Hanon Russell, and Severine Wamala.

Also thanks to Ames Abbott, Gatumba Abu, Donna Alarie, Robert Armes, Ed Astrachan, Sam Atwood, Barry Ball, Michael Barry, Rob Huntington, Robert King, Menno Koning, Jim Krycka, Paul Mishkin, Jeff Penta, Robert Powell, Brad Ryan, Al Ward, the members of the Metrowest Chess Club (www.metrowestchess.org), and my opponents.

# Bibliography

Averbakh, Yuri and Neat, Ken. *Chess Middlegames: Essential Knowledge.* Everyman, 1997.

Blokh, Maxim. *Combinational Motifs.* Convekta Chess, 2000.

Charushin, Victor. *Combination Cross: The Tactician's Handbook.* Pickard & Son, 1998.

Chess Informant. *Anthology of Chess Combinations.* Chess Informant, 1995.

Chess Informant. *Enclopaedia of Chess Middlegames.* Chess Informant, 1980.

Csikszentmihalyi, Mihaly. *Flow: The Psychology of Optimal Experience.* Harper-Collins, 1991.

Dunne, Alex. *How to be a Class A Player.* Thinker's Press, 1987.

Dvoretsky, Mark. *Secrets of Chess Tactics.* Batsford, 1993.

Euwe, Max and Kramer, H. *The Middle Game – Book I.* Hays Publishing, 1994.

Evans, Larry, Silman, Jeremy and Roberts, Betty. *How to Get Better at Chess: Chess Masters on their Art.* Summit Publishing, 1991.

Hays, Lou and Hall, John. *Combination Challenge.* Hays Publishing, 1991.

Heisman, Dan. *Everyone's Second Chess Book.* Thinker's Press, 2000.

Ivaschenko, Sergey. *The Manual of Chess Combinations.* Convekta Chess, 1997.

Keres, Paul, and Kotov, Alexander. *The Art of the Middle Game.* Dover Publications, 1990.

Kotov, Alexander. *Think Like a Grandmaster.* Batsford, 1996.

Lakein, Alan. *How to Get Control of Your Time and Your Life.* New American Library, 1996.

Leonard, George. *Mastery: They Keys to Success and Long-Term Fulfillment.* Plume, 1992.

Livshitz, August. *Test Your Chess IQ: First Challenge.* Everyman, 1997.

Livshitz, August. *Test Your Chess IQ: Master Challenge.* Everyman, 1997.

Livshitz, August. *Test Your Chess IQ: Grandmaster Challenge.* Everyman, 1993.

Neishtadt, Yakov. *Test Your Tactical Ability.* Batsford, 1992.

Nunn, John. *Tactical Chess Endings.* Collier, 1988.

Nunn, John. *John Nunn's Chess Puzzle Book.* Gambit, 1999.

Pandolfini, Bruce. *Pandolfini's Endgame Course.* Simon & Schuster, 1988.

Pandolfini, Bruce. *Chessercizes.* Simon & Schuster, 1991.

Pandolfini, Bruce. *More Chessercizes: Checkmate!.* Simon & Schuster, 1991.

Pandolfini, Bruce. *Beginning Chess.* Simon & Schuster, 1993.

Pandolfini, Bruce. *Chess Target Practice.* Simon & Schuster, 1994.

Pelts, Roman and Alburt, Lev. *Comprehensive Chess Course: Volumes I & II (3rd Revised and Enlarged Edition).* Chess Information and Research Center, 1992.

Polgar, Laszlo and Pandofini, Bruce. *Chess: 5334 Problems, Combinations, and Games.* Black Dog & Leventhal Publishing, 1995.

Pongo, Istvan. *Tactical Targets in Chess Vol 1, Getting a Decisive Material Advantage.* Caissa, 1999.

Pongo, Istvan. *Tactical Targets in Chess Vol 2, Mate Combinations.* Caissa, 1999.

Seirawan, Yasser. *Winning Chess Strategies.* Microsoft Press, 1999.

Seirawan, Yasser and Silman, Jeremy. *Winning Chess Tactics.* Microsoft Press, 1995.

Shamkovich, Leonid and Cartier, Jan. *Tactical Chess Training – 300 Brilliant Tactical Studies from Events 1985-1995.* Hays, 1995.

Silman, Jeremy. *How to Reassess Your Chess: The Complete Chess Mastery Course (Expanded 3rd Edition).* Summit Publishing, 1993.

Silman, Jeremy. *The Amateur's Mind: Turning Chess Misconceptions into Chess Mastery (2nd Edition/Expanded).* Siles Press, 1999.

Vukovic, Vladimir. *The Art of Attack in Chess.* Globe Pequot, 1998.

Weeramantry, Sunil. *Best Lessons of a Chess Coach.* Random House, 1993.

Yermolinsky, Alex. *The Road to Chess Improvement.* Gambit Publications, 2000.

Znosko-Borovsky, Eugene. *Art of Chess Combination.* Dover Publications, 1977.

# Foreword

*You are what you repeatedly do*

This is the only chess book that describes the exact training method that a weak adult class player used to become a strong club player.

This book was born out of my frustration with existing books on how to study chess. As a weak adult class player, I felt that few chess books were right for me. Opening tomes require too much memorisation and endgame books are too recondite. Middlegame strategy is fun to read, but after analysing my games I did not think that I was losing games because I did not understand minority attacks and weak squares.

As a weak player, I consistently lost games to simple oversights: leaving a piece en prise, missing a mate, or losing my queen to a knight fork. I designed a rigorous program to rid my game of these mistakes. By following this program on a daily basis for five months, I gained 400 USCF rating points in my first year of tournament play and almost 300 rating points in my second year of play.

My Rapid Chess Improvement program has three steps:

    1) Improve your chess vision.

    2) Increase your tactical ability.

    3) Learn how to think over the board.

These three steps are covered in the first three chapters of this book.

Is it hard work? Yes, it is. If you follow all of the instructions in this book to the letter, you will spend hundreds of hours studying chess in a five month period.

The fourth chapter in this book is a set of tactical exercises taken from real games between class players. How good do you need to be tactically to beat players of a certain level? This chapter will help you answer this question.

If you are reading this book in a store and are wondering whether to buy it, turn to Chapter 5 and read about the experiences that others have had following the Rapid Chess Improvement approach. Read about how Cuzear Ford went from being a Class D/Class C player for most of his adult life to being a Class B player in a couple of months after implementing the Rapid Chess Improvement regime. Read how David had the best game of his life after doing a few chess vision drills. Read how dozens of players have seen remarkable improvements in their chess playing abilities and then imagine surprising yourself, your friends, and your opponents with your new-found chess skills.

The final chapter of the book provides some preliminary ideas on how to continue studying after you have finished the Rapid Chess Improvement program.

I am eager to hear about you and your experiences with Rapid Chess Improvement. Please write to me at chessimprovement@attbi.com.

Michael de la Maza,
Cambridge, Massachusetts, USA,
March 2002.

# Introduction

Who is this book for? It is primarily for adult class players who are interested in rapid chess improvement. In this book I describe the five-month plan that helped me to gain 700 United States Chess Federation (USCF) points in two years.

What is rapid chess improvement? In my first year of tournament play I improved from 1321 USCF to 1756 USCF and in my second year I improved from 1756 USCF to 2041 USCF (see Figure 1).

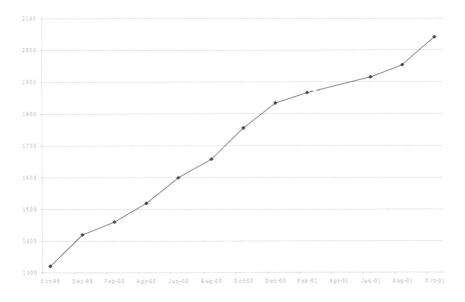

*Figure 1: My chess rating improved from 1321 to 1756 in my first year of play and from 1756 to 2041 in my second year of play.*

I roughly define rapid chess improvement as gaining 200 rating points in 12 months.

I began playing tournament chess in mid-July of 1999. My provisional rating placed me squarely in the Class D category (see Figure 2) because I played, well, like a Class D player. Here are two of my more notable gems:

□ **F.Herman**
■ **de la Maza**
MCC Swiss Under 1700, 1999

**1 e4 c6 2 d4 d5 3 ♘c3 dxe4 4 ♗c4 ♘f6 5 f3 exf3 6 ♘xf3 ♗g4 (Diagram 1) 7 ♗xf7+ ♔d7 8 ♘e5+ Black resigns**

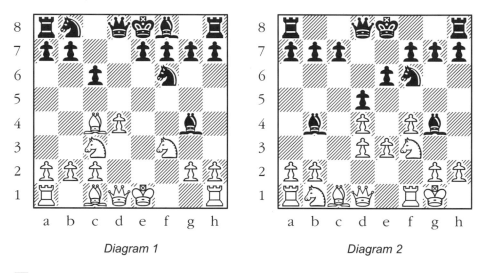

*Diagram 1*                              *Diagram 2*

□ **R.Oresick**
■ **de la Maza**
BCC $12 Open, 1999

**1 d4 d5 2 e3 ♘f6 3 ♗d3 ♘c6 4 f4 ♘b4 5 ♗e2 ♗f5 6 ♗d3 ♘xd3+ 7 cxd3 e6 8 ♘f3 ♗g4 9 0-0 ♗b4 (Diagram 2) 10 ♕a4+ Black resigns**

Dissatisfied with my initial results, I began to search for ways to achieve rapid chess improvement.

I looked at hundreds of book reviews and dozens of books. Unfortunately, the vast majority of these books were either aimed at a much more knowledgeable reader or focused on specific areas, such as openings, which I found arcane and uninteresting.

Discussions with chess coaches were just as unhelpful. Many coaches felt that improving more than 100 rating points in one year was all but impossible for adult players. Others refused to provide me with suitable references. One chess coach who I worked with had me spend a dozen hours on the king, bishop and knight versus king ending in the first month of coaching, and had suggested that I annotate several hundred Grandmaster games in my favourite openings when I decided to stop following his instruction.

| USCF Moniker | USCF | Fide | BCF |
|---|---|---|---|
| Class E | 1000 | 900 | 37.5 |
| Class D | 1200 | 1100 | 62.5 |
| Class C | 1400 | 1300 | 87.5 |
| Class B | 1600 | 1500 | 112.5 |
| Class A | 1800 | 1700 | 137.5 |
| Expert | 2000 | 1900 | 162.5 |
| Master/National Master | 2200 | 2100 | 187.5 |

*Figure 2: USCF/FIDE/BCF conversion. Throughout this book USCF ratings are used. This table converts USCF to FIDE ratings and FIDE to BCF ratings using the following formulae: USCF = FIDE+100; FIDE = 8 x BCF + 600. The USCF ratings given are the minimum ratings required to be of a certain rank. For example, players rated between 1600 and 1799 USCF are Class B players. Players rated below 2000 USCF are collectively called class players.*

As a result of these experiences, I decided to create my own study plan for achieving rapid chess improvement. I followed this plan and improved over 400 points in my first year of tournament play and almost 300 points in my second year of tournament play.

## Shortcomings of Standard Chess Instruction

Devising this study plan, which is based on studying tactics in a particular way, required me to understand why traditional methods of chess tuition were failing.

### Insight number 1: Chess knowledge is not the same as chess ability

When I was researching chess coaches, one comment I often heard from students was: 'I have been studying openings/endgames/middlegames/weak squares/knight outposts and feel that my understanding of the game has improved greatly.' I would always follow these statements with the question: 'So, how much has your rating improved?' Time and time again, students told me that their ratings had not improved in the three months, six months, or year since they had started their coaching.

Why did these students' ratings fail to improve? Class players who spend their time on openings, middlegame strategy and endgames are doing an excellent job of increasing their chess knowledge, but not increasing their chess ability.

For a class player to study openings, middlegame strategy and endgames as a way of increasing chess ability (as opposed to chess knowledge) is the equivalent of fixing a car that doesn't have an engine by polishing the steering wheel: the car looks better, but it still doesn't go.

A class player's chess ability is limited first and foremost by a lack of tactical ability. As GM (Grandmaster) Jonathan Levitt wrote in a KasparovChess.com article: 'At lower levels of play...tactical awareness (or a lack of it) usually decides the outcome of the game...' Or as GM Nigel Davies writes on his web site (www.checkerwise.co.uk): 'In the Minor section of weekend congresses one can witness players trying to ape the openings of players like Kasparov. Other players will desperately try to get their 'surprise' in first through fear of their opponent's 'preparation'. I really find all this quite amazing not least because the games concerned are almost invariably decided much later on and often by rather unsophisticated means.' Kasparov himself has said: 'Openings really don't matter at the beginning level.'

Consider the following thought experiment: Take two Class C players and give one the positional knowledge of a Grandmaster and the other the tactical ability of a Grandmaster and then imagine that they play a game. Who will win? Clearly, the Class C player with the GM's tactical ability will win. After the Class C player with the GM's positional knowledge gets an edge in the opening, he will drop a piece to a five-move combination. In fact, give the Class C player an Expert's tactical ability, rather than a GM's, and he will still win.

You can perform a similar experiment with any chess-playing program: create two personalities, one without any positional knowledge (no opening book, no understanding of pawn structure, etc.) and with the maximum tactical knowledge and the other with the maximum positional knowledge but no tactical knowledge. When these two personalities play against each other, the tactical personality will win every game.

You can refine this experiment further by creating two personalities, one that can see three moves ahead but has no positional knowledge and the other that can see two moves ahead and has complete positional knowledge. The tactical personality, which can see three moves ahead, will win the vast majority of the games.

This is a key lesson: all of the positional knowledge in the world is worth less than the ability to see one move ahead. In other words, given the choice between being able to see five moves ahead in every position and having no positional knowledge and being able to see four moves ahead in every position and having a GM's positional knowledge, you should choose the former.

## Insight number 2: GM instruction is sub-optimal at the class level

'It's generally – but erroneously – assumed that the best teachers are the best players, and that the best players can easily communicate the secrets of the game. Actually, the best teachers are often just interested amateurs...'

*GM Andrew Soltis*

Virtually all chess instruction stems, in one way or another, from material prepared by GMs. Grandmasters, however, have two characteristics that make it difficult for them to communicate effectively with adult class players.

First, almost all GMs were master-level players by the time they became adults. A corollary to this fact is that virtually no GM has experienced rapid chess development as an adult player. I believe that this is why many chess coaches think that it is all but impossible for an adult chess player to improve more than 100 rating points in a year. Since very few chess coaches have ever achieved such improvement, they find it difficult to imagine that anyone else can achieve such success. The fault with this analysis is, of course, that the chess coach is starting from a very high level. The question that adult class players would like to have answered is: How much can a 1300 player expect to improve in a year provided that he or she has a superior study plan?

Second, GMs are so far removed in playing strength from class players that their advice is often misguided. For the same reason that a university mathematics professor will probably not be able to teach addition as well as a first grade teacher, a GM will probably not be able to teach the basics of chess as effectively as a pedagogically inclined player who is much weaker.

IM Jeremy Silman echoes this sentiment when he writes: 'Most tournament players reside in the Class D through Class A range. Just about all of them would love to improve their game, and so they slog through modern books by Schiller, Pandolfini, Silman, Nunn, Dvoretsky and endless other authors. The truth is, many of these writers are so much stronger than the average D-A student that they can't really address their problems, simply because they can no longer relate to them.'

These two facts have created an interesting situation: while some instructors, such as Bruce Pandolfini, are known for their work with young students and others, such as Dvoretsky, are known for their ability to help strong players become world-class players, there are no chess instructors who are known for their ability to help adult class players achieve rapid improvement.

## Insight number 3: Quick fixes work at the class level

Strong chess players like to talk about the many years of dedication and hard work that are required to become a master-level player. Unfortunately, they often confuse this hard and time-consuming path with the relatively small amount of work that most class players need to do to experience a significant improvement in their playing ability.

For example, in Yermolinsky's *The Road to Chess Improvement*, a runner up for the 2000 British Chess Federation Book of the Year award, Yermo spends several pages denigrating simple set-ups such as the Grand Prix Attack. He argues that a chess player must be willing to dedicate a substantial amount of time to studying a 'real' opening. With all due respect to Yermolinsky, this advice is off the mark. A Class D player can become a Class B player in one year without knowing the Sicilian or the Grünfeld or the Ruy Lopez. I know because I did just that. As FM Pelts and GM Alburt write in *Comprehensive Chess Course (Volume II)*: 'We beg students who are addicted to opening manuals to remember that most players who spend their time studying theory never reach A-level.'

Unfortunately, the myth that deep theoretical knowledge is required in order to improve permeates the class player community. I once saw a Class E player carrying around Keres' *The Art of the Middle Game* at a tournament and studying it between rounds. This player would have been better off setting up random positions on the board and looking for tactics.

# The Mythology of Chess Mastery

Once while reading a popular Internet news group, I came across an amazing exchange which illustrates one of the most common myths in chess: that to become an Expert, you must be specially gifted. A novice had posted a request asking for information on how to improve and said, 'My goal is to improve 200 ELO points during the year of 2001 and another 200 points in 2002, reaching an average of 1900-2000 at end of 2002.' Having done something similar myself, I knew that, although difficult, this was certainly within the realm of possibility.

But one respondent wrote: 'Yeah, you and everyone else. Given the information you have given, your goal, while a common one, is unrealistic... Instead of worrying about being an Expert, which you will probably never be, just focus on figuring out the flaws in your game and making improvements on them, and be happy if you one day get to Class A.'

Although a bit more blunt than usual, this answer encapsulates a belief that seems to be quite common amongst adult class players. At the 2000 World Open, the largest tournament in the United States, I participated in the Class B section, and, after losing a game, commented that I would like to be a Master some day. My opponent asked me how old I was (30 at the time) and then said I would never be a Master. I then said that I might settle for being an Expert and he said that was extremely unlikely as well. A year later at the 2001 World Open I became an Expert and achieved a Master-level performance rating.

My personal view, admittedly supported only by anecdotal evidence, is that anyone who can read and write fluently in a language and can ride a bike can become an Expert and probably a Master. This rise to excellence will not happen overnight and will take much effort, but I believe just about everyone that fits this description has the inherent capacity to become a good chess player.

I do not believe, as some do, that to become an Expert you must be born with a special chess gene or start playing at a very young age. My experience – and Chris Dingle's (see Figure 3) – refutes this common belief. I do not believe that a Class D player who has never risen above 1500 his entire adult life cannot improve. I do not believe that Experts and Masters have a mystical skill that cannot be acquired by study. Respected chess author IM John Donaldson seconds this opinion: 'I feel that everyone can get to the expert level... Actually anyone who is willing to work very hard at the game should be able to reach the IM ranks.'

## How Long Should it Take to Become an Expert?

Possibly the strongest argument against the belief that becoming a good chess player requires a special gift is to compare chess to other intellectual disciplines and ask 'What is required to become good in that discipline?'

The data on this subject is very clear: in every intellectual discipline, from Archaeology to Zoology, becoming accomplished is a matter of time, work, and practice, not heavenly intervention. Mounds of empirical data support this claim.

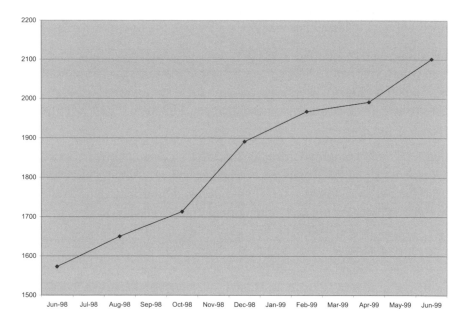

*Figure 3: Adult class player Chris Dingle (USCF ID 12675450) improved from 1573 on 6/98 to 2101 on 6/99, a rate of improvement that is almost double mine.*

Let's work through a calculation that crystallises how much work is required to progress from being a novice to being an accomplished practitioner. If I wanted to learn about archaeology – a subject that I know nothing about – I could take a two-year course at a local university and earn an Associate's degree. After receiving this degree I would certainly know more than 99% of the people in the world about archaeology.

How long would it take to get this degree? Assuming that I take four classes per semester, spend ten hours per week for each class, and each semester lasts fifteen weeks (all very generous assumptions), it would take me 2400 hours (4 semesters x 4 classes/semester x 10 hours/week x 15 weeks/class) to earn my Associate's degree. The actual number of hours is probably half this amount.

Given that a similar argument holds for all other academic disciplines, not just archaeology, it should also apply to chess. Becoming an accomplished chess player should take approximately 2400 hours.

Some might argue that in calculating how long it takes to become an accomplished archaeologist I was comparing myself to the population at large, not just to those who are interested in archaeology and hence the analogy does not apply to chess because chess ratings compare chess players to other chess players and not to the general population.

There is some truth to the statement. However, very few chess players are professionals while someone with an associate's degree in archaeology would certainly be a professional archaeologist and would be far superior to the population of people who are interested in archaeology.

Let's say then that a person with an associate's degree in a particular field is in the top 10% when compared to people who are interested, either as amateurs or professionals, in that field. This will allow a direct comparison to chess ratings.

According to the USCF website, someone who has a rating of 1900 is in the top 7%-11% of all chess players. Hence, according to our calculations, it should take approximately 2400 hours to reach this level and become an accomplished chess player.

This is certainly in line with my experience. It took me about twenty months to achieve a rating of 1900 and during that time I studied two to three hours a day for a total of approximately 1500 hours of study (2.5hrs/day x 30 days/month x 20 months). In addition I played approximately 200 chess games, each of which took a approximately three hours for a total of 2100 hours of study time (1500 hours + 200 games x 3 hours/game).

Note that this argument applies to becoming good, but not great, in a particular discipline. This calculation holds for reaching the top 10% in a population composed of both amateurs and professionals interested in a particular field. To become one of the top human beings in the world – in chess or in any other discipline – a special gift may be needed. But even in this case, several authorities, most notably Laszlo Polgar, would argue that chess perfection is a product of nurture not nature.

There is also one other caveat: to become a top 10% player in 2400 hours of study you need to follow a program of study. A person who wants to receive a degree in archaeology must follow a planned, carefully thought out program of study that includes attending classes, writing papers and doing homework. Randomly examining archaeology texts will not lead to top 10% mastery.

Despite this seemingly obvious fact, many chess players seem to do exactly this – follow a course of random study. Once a chess player learns the rules of the game, there appears to be virtually no clear understanding of how to continue.

How can it be that reading a certain book is good for the Class D player, the Class A player, and the Master. Does this work in any other discipline? Imagine a mathematics textbook being equally informative to someone who has just learned how to count and a university professor.

In this book I describe the exact study plan that I used to improve 400 points in one year. You will no longer have to wonder whether openings should be studied before endgames or endgames before middlegames or middlegames before openings. My study plan lasts five months and for every day during that 150-day period you will know exactly what to do.

To summarise, becoming an Expert or a Master can be achieved over time through hard work – a special gift is helpful but is definitely not necessary. There is no doubt that some people may have a predilection for chess and they will not need to work as hard to achieve a particular rating. However, just about every-one can become an Expert for the same reasons that just about everyone can become a good archaeologist or zoologist.

## Tactics: Get Rid of the Big Squiggly Lines First

Once I understood that many of the beliefs surrounding chess study were incorrect, I wondered if there was a way to study chess that would lead to rapid chess improvement. Improving rapidly was important for my enjoyment of the game. As IM Ignacio Marin notes, '...if you don't improve fast enough the experience will be so painful that you probably will not want to play chess at all after a while.'

An interesting exercise courtesy of Professor Fritz (Fritz is one of the world's most popular computer chess programs and is available from www.chessbase.com) helped to clarify my thinking on what I should study first. I analysed a game of mine that took place when I was a Class C player. My opponent was also a Class C player. The game went through the following phases:

1) The first eight moves were approximately equal.

2) On the ninth move my opponent blundered a knight for two pawns.

3) I maintained my knight for two pawns advantage until the 27th move, when my opponent blundered again giving me an additional pawn.

4) Then on the 29th move I blundered in fantastic fashion and gave my opponent the opportunity to mate.

5) Instead of seeing the mate, my opponent immediately blundered back, giving me an advantage of a full rook.

6) The game continued for another ten moves with both sides regularly making sub-optimal moves.

Fritz's evaluation graph, which shows which side is winning and by how much after every move, has wild swings, indicating that both sides made critical tactical mistakes.

In contrast, a similar exercise done with a GM game, say Shirov-Polgar (Mexico 2000), looks quite different. In this game, which Shirov won, Professor Fritz judges the position to be between +/= (small advantage to White) and =/+ (small advantage to Black) for the first 31 moves of the game, a sharp contrast to the game between the two Class C players which saw five major tactical blunders in the first 30 moves. From move 32 to 39 Black maintains a -/+ (clear) advantage. The advantage switches back and forth until move 43 when Black allows an advanced pawn and the game is over when Black blunders on move 46.

I encourage you to perform this experiment yourself using games involving players of different strengths. You will notice a monotonic relationship between the number of big squiggly jumps in the evaluation function and the players' ratings: the higher the rating, the smaller and fewer the jumps.

Clearly, to become a good player you must reduce the number of material changes that put you at a disadvantage. This is far more important than memorising a deep opening line that will lead to a +/= advantage or learning the bishop, knight and king versus king endgame.

This is the fundamental reason to begin by studying tactics: if the big squiggly lines are going against you, it does not matter how many little squiggly lines are in your favour. Here are some other reasons to focus on studying tactics:

1) Tactical shots are easier to analyse. Suppose that you are reading a book that discusses a position in which positional factors, not tactical ones, are the overriding concern. If you have a question about a variation that is not covered in the book, what can you do? Not much, unless you have a chess coach who is willing to answer questions ad nauseum. In contrast, you can receive GM-level tactical analysis by using a computer and can fully understand every variation.

There is an amusing experiment that you can try in order to verify the difficulty of understanding positional evaluations. Pick any analysed position in Jeremy Silman's *Reassess Your Chess* (the book that has become famous for teaching class players positional concepts), set up the position on your favourite computer program and play the side that is winning according to Silman. After a few moves the computer will deviate from Silman's analysis. Feel free to check Silman's book or any other source for advice on what to do about the computer's 'new idea'. You will quickly learn that the computer has busted Silman's plan and a new plan is required. Now what do you do? If you are a GM you can create a new plan (provided that you didn't reject Silman's plan from the start), but if you are a class player there is little that you can easily do to learn about the new position.

I stress that this is not a comment about Silman or his books. This is a general comment about middlegame strategy and applies to any of the classic middlegame books (*The Art of the Middlegame* by Keres and Kotov; *The Middlegame* by Euwe and Kramer; *Chess Middlegames* by Averbakh). Until you are ready to teach yourself about chess, middlegame strategy should be left untouched. And you are not ready to teach yourself about chess until you stop making three-move tactical errors.

2) Studying tactics gives you many things for free. In particular, you will naturally learn many positional concepts by studying tactics. For example, which is the better way to learn about the benefits of castling: (A) learn a positional 'rule' along the lines of 'castle early' or (B) do ten tactical problems in which a king in the centre of the board gets mated? Clearly (B) is superior. If you come across an opponent who fails to castle early and you know (A) you'll be able to say: 'Jeepers! My opponent doesn't know how to play chess – he didn't castle early.' If you learned about the benefits of castling by following option (B) you will know 10 concrete ways to punish the opponent. The same thing is true of many other positional concepts. What is the best way to learn about colour complexes, knight outposts, gambit openings, rooks on the seventh rank, etc.? At the class level, the best and easiest way is to learn tactics.

National Master Spencer Lower summarises this advantage succinctly: 'Tactical study is not strictly for attack, but aids your positional play. You need to know what to avoid when defending. If you can't see the combination coming at you, you can't milk your positional advantage, or maintain the balance.'

3) Positional understanding requires tactical understanding. Class players may find the right plan in the middlegame only to blunder away a piece because they fail to see a tactical shot. Or they continue pursuing their plan despite the fact that they have an immediate opportunity to win by grabbing an opponent's piece. Positional understanding without tactical ability is worth little.

This leads to an important concept which I like to call 'visibility'. If a particular chess skill is not visible, then you will play as if you did not have it. For example, suppose that you are a Master level endgame player but have a Class E level ability to identify tactics. Your endgame ability will never be visible against any-one rated above 1600 because you will reach the endgame a piece down.

Positional ability is not visible until your tactical ability is in place. Small tactical errors will obscure even the most refined positional skills. Before you advance your game by improving your positional skills, make sure that those skills will be visible in a game by drilling your tactical skills to a level where you are no longer making three-move blunders.

## Answers to Frequently Voiced Objections

I've had the opportunity to share the analysis in this chapter with hundreds of class players and have heard many of their questions and concerns.

One of the most frequently heard objections to focusing on tactics exclusively is: 'In order for a tactical opportunity to arise, positional/middlegame/strategic (PMS) play is required.' This question is asked in many ways, but the core concern of the question is always the same: tactical opportunities do not appear out of thin air, players must work hard to create them.

This may be true at the Master level, but is certainly not true at the class player level. A simple two-step argument suffices to prove this point:

1) Class players know next to nothing about PMS play.

2) Tactical opportunities (and the failure to recognise them) decide virtually every game between class players.

Clearly if PMS abilities were required to create tactical opportunities, both of these statements would not be true.

Another objection I hear is that if openings are not studied with great care, the game is lost immediately and the opportunity to exhibit tactical ability is not pos-sible.

Again, at the Master level there may be a difference between playing an opening that gives you a +/= advantage and one that does not. At the class level, how-ever, a +/= is simply irrelevant. There are too many big squiggly lines in class play for the opening to be of much importance.

If you are dropping pieces in the opening, understand that you do not have an opening weakness, you have a tactical weakness. There is no opening that wins a piece by force, so if you find yourself down a piece by move ten on a regular basis, you should know that you are being outplayed tactically.

A third objection I hear is that studying tactics is no fun. Studying strategic battles is more interesting and enlightening. I must confess that I agree with this objection. I would much rather read a beautiful, novel-like account by Sunil Weeramantry, author of *Best Lessons of a Chess Coach,* of how a game was won than plough through 50 tactical problems. When I first started to study tactics seriously, blood poured from my forehead. However, you must know that if you refuse to study tactics then, to quote GM Miguel Quinteros, you are 'doomed to remain weak' and are 'well advised to take up something else, like knitting.'

## Summary

By now you should be convinced of the material rule in chess: He who has the material, rules. Positional considerations are of little importance when you are dropping pieces.

The best way to capture material and to avoid giving away material at the class level is to study tactics. Opening, middlegame, and endgame study may indirectly improve tactical ability, but why dance with the barmaid when the prom queen is yours for the taking? Opening, middlegame, and endgame ability is of little use when you are dropping pieces and failing to notice when your opponent drops a piece. In *The Amateur's Mind (2nd Edition)*, IM Jeremy Silman writes 'I have noticed that the vast majority of games between amateurs are decided by some gross blunder of material. This means that if you can simply not give anything away (no deep strategy here!) you will see hundreds of points pad your rating.'

After many months of thinking about how to improve in chess, this is the same conclusion I reached: If I could just stop giving material away, my rating would improve by leaps and bounds. In the remaining chapters of this book you will learn the exact study plan that I used to improve 400 points in one year and 700 points in two years.

Tactics work is hard work. But if you are a class player and want to improve you must stop leaving pieces *en prise*, you must be able to see two-move calculations with almost perfect accuracy, and you must be able to regularly see three- and four-move combinations.

# Chapter One

# Chess Vision Drills

In this chapter I discuss several different types of chess vision drills and how to use them to improve your chess playing skills. Two of the drills are part of the core study program while the remainder is optional.

The primary goal of chess vision drills is to enable you to *know* instead of *calculate*. Consider the simple multiplication problem: 45x73. Surely you know how to *calculate* the solution. However, there is a small chance that you will make an error and it will take a bit of time before you know the answer. Instead, if you *know* the answer you will see the solution immediately and you will not make any errors.

Games in the lower sections of tournaments are regularly punctuated by 'Aaargh!!!' and 'Ohh!!' as players slap their foreheads after making one-move blunders. Working on chess vision drills in the way prescribed in this chapter will greatly reduce the frequency of your one-move blunders and will increase your ability to capitalise on your opponent's blunders.

When athletes practice, they repeat short exercises over and over again. For example, basketball players stand at the free throw line and shoot free throw after free throw. Soccer players practice simple passing schemes repeatedly.

Standard chess study involves very few of these micro-level drills but here, in the first step of the study plan, this is exactly what you will be doing. The first step lasts 28 days. During the first 14 days you will practice simple forks and skewers. During the next 14 days you will focus on the knight and how it moves.

# The Two Critical Chess Vision Drills

All chess vision drills have a critical property: they are very simple and hence allow your mind to focus on a single idea. By stripping away the complexity of normal chess positions, chess vision drills help you to improve specific skills without being distracted. In the same way that golf players break their swing down into many different components, by doing chess vision drills you will break down your skills and drill each one to perfection.

One of the problems of studying complete games is that there is so much happening during every position that learning the correct information is very difficult. Although this complexity is part of the beauty of chess, it is often harmful to a chess beginner's health. Chess vision drills solve this problem.

Chess vision drills should be performed in two phases. During the intensive phase, you should repeat each chess vision drill every single day for at least a week. Then during the refresh phase you should repeat the chess vision drill at least once a month and before critical tournaments or games.

## Concentric Square

To practice simple forks and skewers use an exercise that I call the Concentric Square. Begin by placing the black king on d5 and a black rook on d4. Now sequentially place the white queen on every square where it safely forks or skewers the black king and rook. Once you have determined that there are no such squares, move the rook in a square around the king (squares e4, e5, e6, d6, c6, c5, and c4) and look for forks and skewers. When you find such a square, physically lift up the white queen and place it on the square. Involving your body in this process is critical because it helps to cement the connection between the position and the key square. Note that positions in which the black king can recapture the queen after the queen captures the rook are not valid. Focus only on positions in which the capture of the rook is safe.

Now move the rook one square further away from the king and repeat the process. The rook now moves through the squares c3, d3, e3, f3, f4, f5, f6, f7, e7, d7, c7, b7, b6, b5, b4, and b3. Continue moving the rook one more square away from the king until the rook reaches the edge of the board. See Figure 4 for the path that the rook traces as it moves in concentric squares around the king.

Now replace the black rook on d4 with a black bishop, black knight, and black queen and repeat the Concentric Square exercise.

Finally, pound the attacking patterns into your brain by repeating the Concentric

Square exercise for each of the black pieces (black rook, black bishop, black knight, and black queen) every day for fourteen days.

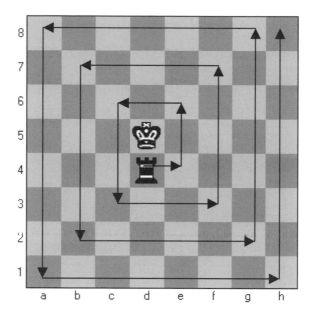

*Figure 4: This figure illustrates the concentric squares that the rook traces as it moves around the stationary king. The rook travels the following path: d4, e4, e5, e6, d6, c6, c5, c4, c3, d3, e3, f3, f4, f5, f6, f7, e7, d7, c7, b7, b6, b5, b4, b3, b2, c2, d2, e2, f2, g2, g3, g4, g5, g6, g7, g8, f8, e8, d8, c8, b8, a8, a7, a6, a5, a4, a3, a2, a1, b1, c1, d1, e1, f1, g1, h1, h2, h3, h4, h5, h6, h7 and h8.*

By the end of these fourteen days your ability to see forks and skewers in your first ten-second glance at the board will vastly improve. After the initial 14-day period, consider going through these exercises once or twice a week and before games to refresh your skills. You can add variety to these exercises by using a white rook, knight, or bishop instead of a white queen and changing the position of the black king to, say, g8 and c8, the two squares that the king moves to after castling.

As you are going through these exercises you will probably notice that the knight poses the most difficulty. The squares that the other pieces can move to just pop out while the squares that the knight moves to often have to be 'calculated' by class players. This consumes time and energy that could be used on other aspects of the game. When I was a Class D player I remember dreading having an opponent's knight posted on e5/e4/d5/d4 because I knew that I would overlook a fork at some point. Conversely, I knew that if I was able to post a knight on one of the four centre squares, I was very likely to win the game.

## Knight Sight

The next micro drill, which I call Knight Sight, is designed to make the squares that a knight can move to 'pop out'. Begin by placing a knight on a1 and physically hit the squares that it can move to (c2 and b3) with your finger (see Figure 5). Then move the knight to a2 and repeat the process. Continue until you reach a8 and then move back to b1, going row by row until you reach h1. Repeat this Knight Sight exercise every day for one week.

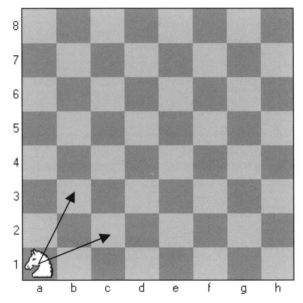

*Figure 5: Improve your Knight Sight by placing the knight on a1 and then physically hitting the squares that it can move to, c2 and b3, with your finger. Then move the knight to a2 and repeat the process.*

At the end of this week, test your Knight Sight by placing the knight on random squares on the board and see if the squares that it can move to jump out at you. If not, repeat the process for another week and continue doing so until you no longer need to calculate the knight's moves.

Once your Knight Sight meets your standards, you are ready to move on to the next step. Place a knight on d5 and calculate the minimum number of moves that it takes to bring the knight to d4 (see Figure 6). You can prove that it takes exactly three moves: first you can show that it does not take one move because your Knight Sight makes the squares that the knight can move to in one move pop out, and d4 is not one of them. Second, you know that it cannot take two moves to move the knight to d4 because the knight alternates colours, and since d5 is a dark square, it cannot be on d4 which is a light square after two moves. Third, it does not require more than three moves to go from d5 to d4 because you can calculate at least one path (e.g., d5-c3-e2-d4) that takes exactly three moves.

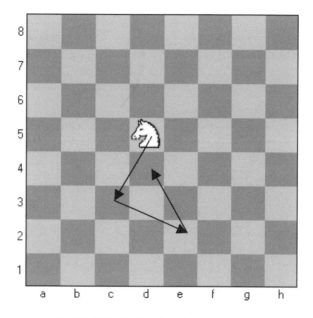

*Figure 6: Improve your Knight Sight further by placing the knight on d5 and calculating the shortest path to d4. For added challenge, calculate all minimal paths.*

Now go through the same process that we followed in the Concentric Squares micro drill. Starting each exercise with the knight on d5, move the knight to the squares e4, e5, e6, d6, c6, c5, and c4 in the minimal number of moves. For added challenge find all of the minimal paths, not just one. Now, just as before, expand the concentric square as shown in Figure 4 and repeat the process. Continue expanding the square until the knight is at the edge of the board.

Repeat this process every day for a week. As a refresher, repeat it before tournaments and on a monthly basis. You can vary the exercise by changing the knight's starting square. Instead of d5, try c3, f3, b1, and g1 – all natural squares for the knight.

Some players may object that these micro drills are so trivial that they are unnecessary. The fact that they are trivial, however, does not mean that they are not useful. Remember that soccer players practice penalty kicks and basketball players practice slam-dunks even though these tasks are trivial. Professional athletes perform these micro drills over and over again so that they can perform at a high level in adverse situations.

Even very strong players sometimes make simple Chess Vision mistakes. For example, GM Joel Benjamin missed a mate in one against Boris Gulko at the 2000 US Championships. The purpose of these exercises is to automate the knowledge that you already have so that you unconsciously see simple combinations without having to exert any effort. The time and energy that you save can then be spent on calculating more complicated combinations.

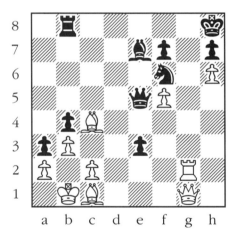

*Benjamin-Gulko, 2000 US Championships. Benjamin is winning but here he played 32 ♗xe3?? allowing 32...♛b2 mate.*

After working through these micro drills, you are now finished with step one of the five-month course. Your ability to spot simple combinations and to calculate knight moves will have greatly improved.

If you feel that your chess vision skills still need to be bolstered, continue to do the drills until you are comfortable and satisfied with your skills. You can also supplement these exercises with the optional chess vision drills that are discussed in the next section. Remember that a significant fraction of the errors that are made in the lower levels of chess tournaments are the simple one move mistakes that can easily be eliminated by doing chess vision drills on a regular basis.

# Optional Chess Vision Drills

In this section I describe additional chess vision drills that you can use to further develop your abilities. These drills are very helpful, even for strong players. Use them if you feel that you are missing obvious opportunities or are taking too much time to find simple moves.

## Knight Flight

Knight Flight is the grown up version of Knight Sight. Instead of moving the knight along the shortest path between adjacent squares, you will work on being able to see the shortest path between any two squares.

To execute the Knight Flight drill, start with the knight on a1 and move it to b1 in the shortest number of moves, just as in the Knight Sight drill. As with the Knight Sight drill, physically hit the squares that the knight moves to, but do not move the knight itself.

Once you have completed the a1-b1 circuit, move the knight from a1 to c1. The shortest path is now just two moves: b3-c1. As before, physically hit the b3-square and the c1-square with your finger.

With the knight still on a1 continue through the standard loop, going through all of the squares on the board. What is the maximum number of moves that it takes to move a knight from a1 to any other square on the board? You should be able to answer this question after completing this drill.

After you have completed all of the circuits that start on a1 and go to all of the other squares on the board (b1-h1; h2-a2; a3-h3; h4-a4; a5-h5; h6-a6; a7-h7; h8-a8), move the knight to b1 and repeat the process. Once you have gone through all of the squares, move the knight to the c1-square and repeat the process. Then cycle through all of the remaining squares on the board. By the end of this drill you will have placed the knight on every square on the board and from each square you will have moved the knight to every other square on the board.

This drill will take half a day to complete. There are a total of 4032 (64*63) pairs of squares on the board and, assuming that it takes 5 seconds to complete one path, it will take over 5 hours (4032*5/3600) to work through the entire drill.

The ability to quickly know how to move a knight from any square on the board to any other square will have a marked effect on your chess vision, particularly in endgames which feature knights.

The diagram below shows an example from one of my own games. With Black to move, Fritz judges the position to be approximately equal. But my opponent, an experienced 1800 player, was not able to move his knight as effectively as I did. Play continued as follows: 27...♘a7 28 ♘c3 ♘c8 29 ♘e4 f5 30 ♘c5 ♛xd6 31 ♘e6+ ♛xe6 32 ♛xd8 and Black resigned in two more moves. In this sequence I moved my knight effectively four times in just four moves, something that I would not certainly have been able to do without the benefit of the Knight Flight micro drill.

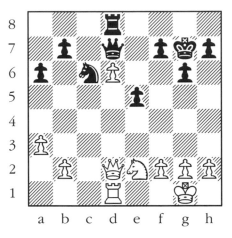

*The Knight Flight micro drill will improve your ability to quickly evaluate positions in which knights play a major role. In this example, my opponent (Black) is an experienced 1800 player. Fritz judges this position to be equal. Play continued: 27...♘a7 28 ♘c3 ♘c8 29 ♘e4 f5 30 ♘c5 ♛xd6 31 ♘e6+ ♛xe6 32 ♛xd8 and Black resigned in two more moves.*

As with all other micro-drills, the Knight Flight drill needs to be repeated on successive days to be effective. Ideally, during the initial intensive phase, you will go through the Knight Flight drill twice a day for two weeks. During the refresh phase you will go through the Knight Flight drill at least once a month and before significant tournaments and games.

## Pawn Grab

This drill will help you to see the quickest way to move your pieces to capture your opponent's pawns. This drill is particularly useful for rook and pawn endings.

To work this drill place a white rook on a square and then place any number of black pawns on the board (see the diagram below).

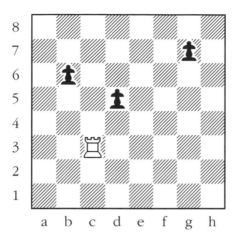

*An example set-up for the pawn capture drill*

Now, in your mind's eye, calculate the shortest number of moves required for the rook to capture all of the black pawns. Now move the rook to each square on the board and repeat the process.

After you have gone through each square on the board with this particular pawn set-up you should notice many patterns. What is the minimal number of moves required to capture all of the pawns? Are there any squares that are particularly hard? These are all questions that are of critical importance in rook and pawn endgames.

You can now change the configuration of the black pawns and repeat the process. You can create variations of this drill by changing the white rook to another piece (the knight is, as usual, particularly difficult).

After spending at least a week on this drill, concentrate on variations that are cropping up in your games. Are you reaching many rook and pawn positions in which there are six or seven pawns on the board? Then drill those positions. Are you reaching positions in which a bishop plays a critical role? Then work on bishop pawn grab drills.

## Pawn Mines

The Pawn mines drill is the opposite of the pawn grab drill. Instead of focusing on capturing pawns you now focus on moving a piece to a target square without landing on any square that a pawn attacks.

For an example, see the diagram below. What is the minimal number of moves the rook must make to reach h5 without landing on a square where it can be captured by a black pawn? Note that h3-h5 does not work because on h3 the rook can be captured by the g4 pawn. Another two-move path, c5-h5, does not work because on c5 the rook can be captured by the b6 pawn.

The shortest number of moves is three. The path c2-h2-h5 is an example, as are c1-h1-h5 and c8-h8-h5. Are there any others? For this drill you should focus on finding all minimal paths.

As with other drills, once you have found the solution, you should move the key piece, in this case the rook, to another square on the board and repeat the exercise. As you find more solutions with the same pawn set-up you will start to notice patterns and you will get faster and faster at finding a solution.

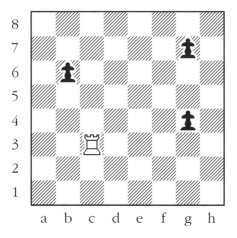

*What is the minimal number of moves that the white rook must make to reach h5 without landing on a square where it can be captured by a pawn?*

Try this drill with various pieces. In the diagram, if the rook is changed to a queen how many moves does it take to get to h5?

## King Attack

The king attack chess vision drill improves your ability to directly attack the king. After you finish this drill your ability to finish off attacks when the opposing king is exposed will be greatly improved.

Place a white queen and a black king on the board. Put some pawns in front of the black king (see the diagram below). Now move the queen in the minimal number of moves to a position where it checks the king and cannot be captured.

In the diagram there are many possible two-move solutions: e4-e8, e2-e8, b2-h8, f5-f8, f2-f8, and g6-e8 are just some of them.

Once you have found a solution, move the queen to another square on the board and repeat the process. Continue to do this until you have a calculated a check from every square on the board.

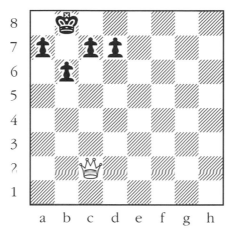

*Learn to attack the king. How many times does the queen have to move before it can check the king?*

As usual you can change the drill by replacing the white queen with a rook, bishop, or a knight. You can make the problem substantially harder by adding a black piece that can block or capture the white piece. Do not move this extra black piece; simply do not allow the white queen to move to a square where it can be captured. Practice this variant only after you have done the basic exercise every day for at least one week.

## Square Name

This drill is particularly helpful for beginners. When I look at the scoresheets of my early games they are riddled with errors. How to fix this problem? Learn the name and colours of the squares.

Look at a chessboard with no pieces and let your eyes fall on a square. Instantly say the name of the square. Repeat the exercise for fifteen minutes a day for at least two weeks until there is no hesitation.

This exercise will reduce the errors on your scoresheets and make it easier to remember long sequences of moves as you familiarise yourself with the board.

Once you have learned the names of the squares, create a set of flash cards with the square name on the front and the colour on the back (see Figure 7). Run through these flash cards until you can instantly say whether a square is dark or light.

*Figure 7: Create flash cards with the name of the square on the front (see left) and the colour on the back (see right). Go through the cards until you can instantly say the colour of a square.*

## How to Create your own Chess Vision Drills

Now that you have seen several examples of chess vision drills, you understand that the essential feature of a chess vision drill is its simplicity. The goal is to strip away the complexity that is usually present on the chessboard and focus on just one concept at a time. Once that feature has been isolated and a chess vision drill is created that captures that feature, the drill is repeated over and over.

As long as you follow these steps – simplification followed by repetition – you can create your own chess vision drills to work on weaknesses in your game.

The diagram below features a position that I played when I was still coming to understand the importance of chess vision drills. I was winning this position very easily but as a weak player I was still concerned that my opponent's two rooks combined with the odd position of my king would cause problems. I was expecting 32 ♖b1 with the idea of doubling rooks down the d-file.

But my opponent played 32 ♖bb2 and resigned immediately after 32...♛xb2

♖xb2 33 ♗xb2. Clearly, my opponent didn't see the double capture on b2. By simplifying the position to a rook and bishop versus a bishop, he eliminated any possibility of rescuing the position.

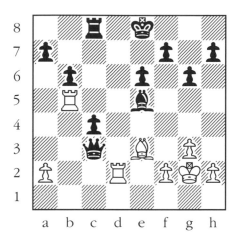

*White played 32 ♖bb2 allowing liquidation on b2: 32...♛xb2 ♖xb2 33 ♗xb2 and White re-signed. White should have kept pieces on with the goal of creating complications.*

How can you create a chess vision drill to help you quickly see double captures like this one?

Begin by identifying the key elements of the position:

    1) Two black pieces are attacking a single square (the 'focal' square).

    2) One white piece is protecting the focal square and the other is on the focal square.

    3) Black captures on the focal square twice.

    4) The piece that Black loses is worth less than the two pieces that White loses.

Once you have identified the key elements, create a simple position with just these elements (see the following diagram).

Check to make sure that all of the key elements are present:

    1) The black queen and bishop are attacking b2, the focal square.

    2) One of white's two rooks is attacking the focal square and the other is on the focal square.

3) Black will capture twice on the focal square, first with the queen and then with the bishop.

4) The piece that Black loses – the queen – is worth less than the two rooks that White loses.

*The key motif*

Because this is a more complicated chess vision drill than the ones given above, there are many dimensions that can be changed

1) The position of the white rook that is protecting the focal square can be changed

2) The position of the black queen and black bishop can be changed.

3) The focal square can be changed.

4) The pieces can all be changed. For example, one of the white rooks could be changed to a white queen.

5) The pieces can be rotated in various ways.

Remember that all chess vision drills should be made as simple as possible. They are *drills* not *problems*. The fewer the dimensions, the easier it will be for your mind to remember.

So let's choose to work first with the focal square. The focal square will rotate through the entire board (a1-h1, h2-a2, a3-h3 etc.) just as the knight moved in the second knight sight drill. (Note that because this drill involves more space, you will not be able to move the focal square to all of the squares on the board.

The focal square cannot be on h8, for example, because there is no room for the other pieces.) You will then move your hand and capture the rook on the focal square with the queen and in your mind's eye imagine the second white rook recapturing on the focal square followed by the black bishop recapturing on the focal square.

At the end of this series of recaptures you should picture the black bishop on the focal square and no other pieces on the board.

As with the other chess vision drills, do this drill several times every day for at least one week. Then refresh your chess vision by doing it several times a month. Before important tournaments and games, you may want to schedule a particularly intensive session in which you go through all of your personal chess vision drills.

Changing the position of the focal square is just one of the many ways that the original motif can be modified. Another way to change the motif is to rotate the pieces around the focal square and then move the focal square through its customary circuit. One such rotation is shown in the diagram below.

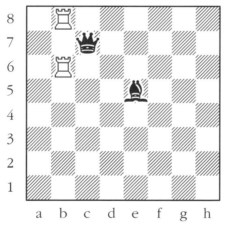

*The key motif has been rotated.*

How many of these variants should you do for every motif that you find troublesome? The answer to this question depends primarily on the gravity of the problem and the amount of time you have.

If you notice that you make the same mistake over and over again, then you should try to drill as many variants as possible, time permitting.

## Summary

Impatient chess players often ask me if doing chess vision drills is absolutely essential. The answer is YES!!! Unless your rating is already above 1800, doing chess vision drills is critical to becoming a strong chess player quickly.

Players sometimes make the mistake of thinking that chess vision drills can be ignored because they are so simple. But remember you are not training for a situation in which you are sitting in the comfort of your living room next to a roaring fire and sipping a glass of cognac. You are training for the fifth hour of the fifth game of a weekend tournament. At that point your ability to instantly see simple errors in your opponent's play and the ability to catch errors in your own play before they occur will significantly increase your rating.

The ability to instantly see simple combinations and calculate simple piece movements is a requirement for mastering more sophisticated combinations. After you have done these chess vision drills you will notice that you are able to spend more time thinking about multi-move combinations and less time checking to make sure that none of your pieces are en prise. You will notice that you can jump on your opponent's mistakes very quickly and that you rarely fail to miss a one-move winner.

These improvements in your chess ability alone will improve your rating markedly. But to achieve these improvements you must follow the guidelines given in this chapter religiously.

# Chapter Two

# The Seven Circles

Now that you have worked on chess vision, you will focus on improving your calculation and recognition skills. As FM Ken Smith says, 'Until you are at least a high Class A player, your first name is 'tactics', your middle name is 'tactics', and your last name is 'tactics'.'

If you have never worked hard to improve your chess, then over the next 127-day period you will. If you have never worked hard at anything, then you will discover the great pleasure of intense focus and concentration. If you feel that you are unable to dedicate enough time to this effort, then I recommend a time management book such as the top rated *How to get control of your time and your life* by Alan Lakein. You might also read *Flow: The Psychology of Optimal Experience* by Mihaly Csikszentmihalyi and *Mastery: The Keys to Success and Long-Term Fulfilment* by George Leonard to get a better understanding of what is required to achieve success in any field. If you are able to follow the Seven Circles improvement strategy, you will experience a vast improvement in your calculation and pattern recognition ability in a four-month period.

Before starting the Seven Circles exercise you will need to gather approximately 1000 tactical problems, ranked in order of difficulty. You will then go through this set seven times. You will take 64 days to make the first pass through all of the problems, averaging approximately sixteen problems per day. Then you will cut the amount of time to 32 days and go through the problems again. You will repeat this process five more times and end up doing all 1000 problems in one day.

During the first four circles, when you will be going through the problems in 64, 32, 16, and 8 days, you will be improving your calculation ability. During the last three circles, when you will go through the problems in four days, two days, and one day, you will be improving your pattern recognition ability.

The 1000 tactical problems should have the following properties:

1) You should work through the problems in order of increasing difficulty. The problems should begin with simple one-move mates and two-move combinations and progress to 7-8 move mates and combinations.

2) They should be from real games.

3) The solutions should have a minimal number of errors. Computer checked problems and solutions are always preferred.

4) The problems should contain mates and combinations to win material.

# CT-ART 3.0: A Great Program for Seven Circles

I found the problems in the CT-ART 3.0 chess software program (www.chessassistant.com) to be ideal for the Seven Circles program. In addition to possessing the four aforementioned properties, CT-ART is also a great teaching tool and has a built-in chess program. The teaching tool provides hints when errors are made and the built-in chess program is available to analyse alternate variations. I found that CT-ART saved me hundreds of hours since I did not have to enter complicated positions manually into a chess program when I failed to understand the solutions. A CT-ART demo is available from the Chess Assistant web site. Note that CT-ART 3.0 comes with 1209 tactical puzzles and in the Seven Circle schedules that I give below that is the number I assume.

The power of CT-ART 3.0 can be shown by stepping through an example. The opening screen for every problem looks like Figure 8. If you make an incorrect first move, then a screen like Figure 9 is shown. This screen highlights the key squares, pieces, and lines of attack in the problem. Unlike a book or many tactics programs, CT-ART does not give you the complete answer to the problem immediately. Instead it effectively gives you a hint. If you make yet another error then CT-ART shows a small and simple version of the problem on a 5x5 screen (see Figure 10). Once again, CT-ART gives you the opportunity to solve the problem without giving away the full answer. CT-ART has even more hint mechanisms than the ones shown here. For example, it will flash the piece that needs to be moved if you continue to make mistakes. Once you get the idea, CT-ART steps you through the combination move by move (Figure 11, Figure 12 and Figure 13). One feature of CT-ART is that it contains almost all of the critical variations (Figure 14), thus forcing you to completely solve the problem.

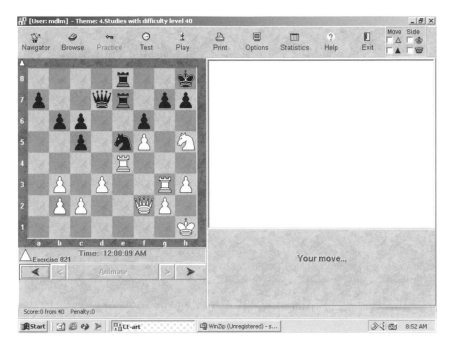

Figure 8: CT-ART displays the starting position of the problem. The white triangle just below the lower left corner of the board means that it is White to move.

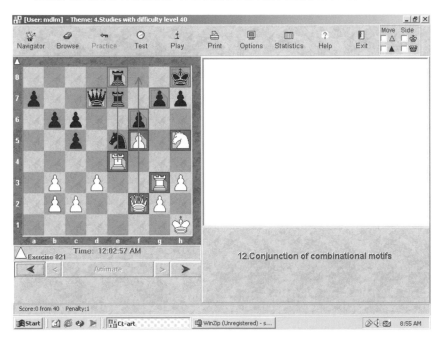

Figure 9: CT-ART shows the key squares, key pieces, and key lines of attack if you make an error. This helps you to solve the problem without giving away the solution.

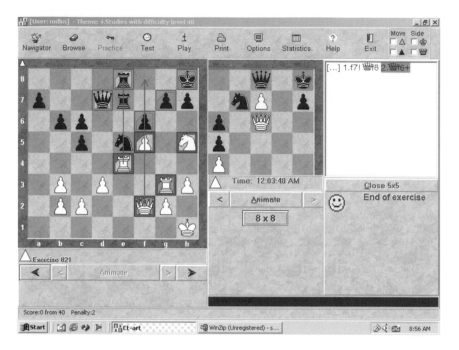

Figure 10: CT-ART gives you the opportunity to solve a simpler version of the problem in a 5x5 window. These simple problems help to reinforce the main tactical ideas.

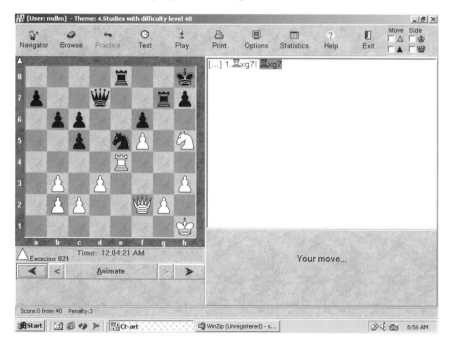

Figure 11: Once you have correctly calculated the first move CT-ART asks for the second.

*Figure 12: CT-ART asks for the third move.*

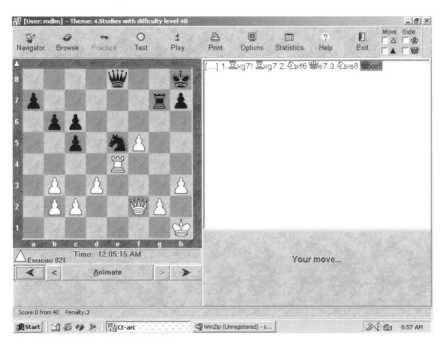

*Figure 13: CT-ART asks for the fourth move.*

Figure 14: CT-ART asks the user to calculate an important variation.

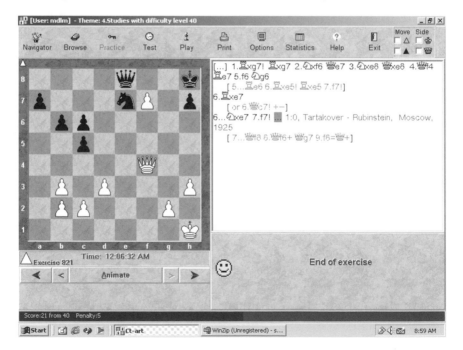

Figure 15: The final screen shows all of the variations as well as your score in the left corner.

Once you are finished with the problem, CT-ART shows your score and the number of mistakes that you made in the lower left-hand corner (see Figure 15). At any time during the problem you can click on Play in the top menu bar and CT-ART will let you play the position from either side against a strong computer chess program, such as Crafty (see Figure 16).

*Figure 16: With one mouse click CT-ART lets you play any position against a strong chess computer program (in this case Crafty).*

## Alternatives to CT-ART 3.0

If you do not have access to a computer you should make every effort to get one. New computers can be purchased with a monitor for under $400 and used computers can be purchased with a monitor for under $200. The money you spend will be immediately returned to you when you start winning prizes at tournaments.

Not having a computer may double the amount of time that it takes to get through Seven Circles. Since Seven Circles takes at least 200 hours you are valuing your time at less than two dollars an hour if you don't pony up the money to buy a computer.

Once you have a computer, install ChessBase Light (from www.chessbase.com)

or one of the many other free chess programs that lets you enter a position and analyse it with a powerful computer chess engine. This will help you understand and analyse tactical positions.

If, for whatever reason, you absolutely cannot get access to a computer, you can, as a last resort, solve problems directly from a book. Please be advised that this option is far inferior to using CT-ART 3.0. Here are some books that I know to be adequate for this purpose:

*Combinational Motifs* by Blokh. If you must buy a book, buy this one. CT-ART 3.0 is based on this tome. This book is difficult to find but it is often available at http://store.convekta.com. Unfortunately, it is arranged by theme so you will have to jump around the book to order the puzzles by difficulty. Solve this problem by photocopying the book and then cutting out the tactical puzzles and rearranging them by difficulty.

*The Manual of Chess Combinations* by Sergey Ivashchenko. Good introductory book with over 1,300 positions.

*Chessercizes*, *More Chessercizes: Checkmate!*, *Chess Target Practice*, and *Beginning Chess*, all books by Bruce Pandolfini. Pandolfini is one of the best (if not the best) chess author for beginners. He is most often associated with scholastic players, particularly Josh Waitzkin of *Searching for Bobby Fischer* fame, but the adult player can also benefit from reading his books. If you are 1200 or below, you might want to consider starting with a collection of Pandolfini books. They tend to have only a few hundred tactical problems each so you will need a handful to collect 1000 problems. The main shortcoming of this approach is that ordering the problems by difficulty is not easy. You will have to do considerable homework before you start Seven Circles and then you will need to jump from book to book during the actual Seven Circles exercises.

*Combination Challenge* by Hays and Hall. A decent book for intermediate players. Many exercises have errors in their solutions, however, so having access to a computer program is very helpful. The book's best feature is that it has over 1000 problems.

*Test Your Chess IQ: First Challenge*, *Test Your Chess IQ: Master Challenge*, *Test Your Chess IQ: Grandmaster Challenge* by August Livshitz. A worthwhile series but make sure that the problems are suitable for you. Personally, I find the *First Challenge* too easy and the *Master Challenge* too difficult so combining the tactics in both books, something that is necessary in any case to collect 1000 problems, may be the best strategy for the typical class player.

*Test Your Tactical Ability* by Neishtadt. Great collection of problems; unfortunately they are arranged by theme, instead of difficulty. Good for intermediate players.

*Tactical Chess Training* by Shamkovich. Great book for intermediate players, but there are only 300 problems, so it must be supplemented.

*Tactical Targets in Chess Vol. 1, Vol. 2* by Pongo. The second volume focuses solely on mating combinations so you should not use it exclusively. An excellent pair of books with lots of explanation and approximately 1000 problems each.

*Chess: 5334 Problems, Combinations, and Games* by Laszlo Polgar with an Introduction by Bruce Pandolfini. This is a book that can be geared to the beginner or to the intermediate player depending on the selection of 1000 problems. All 1000 problems can be simple one or two move combinations or you can choose harder multi-move problems if you are more advanced. If you are not quite sure of your ability or want to have a book that will grow with you, this is the book to buy. One disadvantage of this book is that the solutions to the tactical problems do not show the complete variations.

*Anthology of Chess Combinations* and *Encyclopaedia of Chess Middlegames* by Chess Informant (http://www.sahovski.com). Two similar books with significant overlap. For advanced players only. An electronic edition of *Anthology of Chess Combinations* is available. This is a good follow-on chess package after you have completed CT-ART 3.0. *Encyclopaedia* is older and will be more difficult to find.

Note that even the best of these options is significantly inferior to solving problems on a computer. Many of the books, such as Pandolfini's, do not meet the four requirements suggested above. ChessBase (www.chessbase.com) has several tactics CDs available, the best known of which is *Intensive Course Tactics* by Renko. CT-ART 3.0 is head and shoulders above all of these CDs.

There are several classic chess books, such as *Art of Attack in Chess* by Vukovic, *The Art of Chess Combination* by Znosko-Borovsky, and *Secrets of Chess Tactics* by Mark Dvoretsky, that are not well suited for the Seven Circles exercise. These books contain a lot of high-level theory and explanation, instead of problems. Delve into these books only after you have completed the Seven Circles exercise and have a firm grounding in basic tactics. There are also some very specialised combination books, such as *Combination Cross* by Charushin which, although entertaining and instructive, are so narrowly focused that they will not help you improve your recognition ability nearly as much as a book that contains tactical puzzles with many different motifs.

Also note that there is an entirely different class of puzzles, called problems, which are hand-crafted. Although books on this subject, such as *Anthology of 2345 Chess Problems,* may increase your appreciation for chess, you should stay away from them during the Seven Circles exercises. Because these problems are not from real games and are designed primarily to be intellectually interesting instead of practically useful, they will not help you nearly as much as studying real tactical problems from real games.

## How to Create your own Schedules

Creating and keeping a schedule is one of the critical components of the Seven Circles program. Remember that you will be going through all 1000 problems seven times. The first time you will solve all of the problems in 64 days, then you will solve all of the problems in 32 days, sixteen days, eight days, four days, two days, and one day.

If you do not have the discipline to keep a schedule, then you will not be successful. In *How to Get Control of Your Time and Your Life*, Alan Lakein writes: 'Control starts with planning. Planning is bringing the future into the present so that you can do something about it now.'

Before you start on the Seven Circles program you should have a fully worked out schedule – for all 127 days – so that you know exactly what you will be doing every single day. Make sure that any holidays and vacations have been appropriately accounted for – surprises interfere with effective planning.

Creating your schedule so that you can comfortably go through all of the problems during the first circle, and then through all of the Seven Circles, is critical.

You must first have an understanding of how quickly it takes you to solve problems. How long does it take you to solve the typical two-move puzzle? The three-move checkmate? The queen sacrifice?

Then, you must have a good understanding of the problems that you are going to be doing during the Seven Circles. Go through them and maybe do a few of them to quantify your abilities.

Once you have this information, create a schedule – one for each of the seven circles – that allows you to comfortably solve the problems and spend approximately the same amount of time per day on tactical puzzles. You can schedule days that give you a bit of a break, but you should solve tactical problems every day for the 127-day period. I particularly liked to reduce the number of problems at the end of each Seven Circle to give myself a mini-vacation.

Typically, the number of problems that you do per week during the first few cycles should not decline by more than a factor of two. For example, if you do 200 problems the first week, you should do at least 100 during the next week. And, of course, since the problems are becoming more difficult, the number of problems per week should decline.

I used the Microsoft Excel spreadsheet to create the schedules for many of the schedules. It helped me to see the effect of many different schedules quickly.

## How Much Time to Take per Problem

In order to blast through thousands of tactical problems during the Seven Circles not only do you need to keep to a tight schedule of solving problems; you must also very carefully regiment the amount of time per problem.

If you are using a computer program to work through the tactical puzzles as I recommend above, then the program will keep track of time for you – yet another advantage of using your cybernetic friend. If you are doing the problems from a book, then you should use an egg timer or a countdown timer.

During the first circle, you should take no more than ten minutes per problem. The first five minutes should be used to find the solution and the second five should be used to study the solution. You must keep to a strict time schedule in order to plough through all of the problems in a reasonable amount of time so do not let yourself spend any extra time on each problem. You must also train yourself to solve the tactical problems quickly because under normal game time controls you will usually only have a few minutes per move.

As I noted above, you should not have any difficulty completing the initial problems in your 1000 problem block within ten minutes. If you are encountering problems, then the tactical puzzles you have chosen are too difficult. If needed, start off with several hundred one-move mates and combinations to make sure that you can stay under the ten-minute limit.

Divide the ten minutes per problem in half when you begin the 32-day circle and in half again when you start the 16-day circle. Continue cutting the time in half until you reach the 4-day circle. At this point you will be working through each problem (including reading through the solution) in 37.5 seconds. For the 2-day circle reduce this time to 30 seconds. During the 1-day circle you should also do each problem in 30 seconds. See Figure 17 for the maximum time that you should spend on any problem during each stage of the Seven Circles.

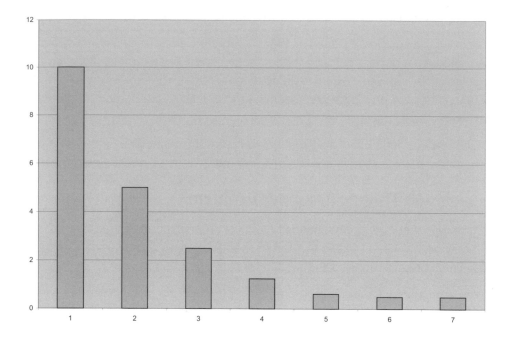

*Figure 17: Maximum time in minutes that you should spend on a problem. During the first circle, for example, you should spend a maximum of ten minutes per problem (including understanding the solution) and in the last circle you should spend a maximum of thirty seconds per problem.*

The last two circles require special dedication. If you are doing 1000 problems then you will be averaging 500 per day in the 2-day circle. At a rate of 30 seconds per problem, you will spend 4 hours and 10 minutes doing tactics problems on each of these two days. In the 1-day circle you will spend 8 hours and 20 minutes doing tactics problems.

Although these last three days are likely to be painful, do not skimp. They are a critical part of the Seven Circles training. You may feel faint, nauseous, and sick. Blood may start dripping from your forehead. But if you have the courage to push on, you will be rewarded with a greatly enlarged tactical muscle that will leave your opponents in the dust.

At the end of the Seven Circles training you will have spent a total of 155 days (28 days doing micro-level drills plus 127 days doing Seven Circles) working on your tactical training ability. If you work through the program exactly as I've described it, your tactical ability will soar.

## My Schedule

In this section I give you an example of the schedules that I used to go through CT-ART 3.0. Be advised that CT-ART has 1209 problems so the schedules were created to give me the time to solve that many problems.

When I started the Seven Circles program I created a list of seven schedules – one for each circle. The schedule for the first circle is shown in Figure 18 and the number of problems that I did every week is shown graphically in Figure 19.

| Week number | Per week | Per day | Total completed | End date |
|:---:|:---:|:---:|:---:|:---:|
| 1 | 233 | 33.3 | 233 | Apr 9th |
| 2 | 203 | 29.0 | 436 | Apr 16th |
| 3 | 174 | 24.9 | 610 | Apr 23rd |
| 4 | 145 | 20.7 | 755 | Apr 30th |
| 5 | 117 | 16.7 | 872 | May 7th |
| 6 | 110 | 15.7 | 982 | May 14th |
| 7 | 93 | 13.3 | 1075 | May 21st |
| 8 | 76 | 10.9 | 1151 | May 28th |
| 9 | 58 | 7.3 | 1209 | Jun 5th |

*Figure 18: Seven Circles 64-day study plan. This table shows my schedule for the first 64-day circle.*

As you will see from the table in Figure 18, in the first week I did a total of 233 problems, approximately 33 per day. In the second week I did a total of 203 problems at the rate of approximately 29 per day. I created a schedule that reduced the number of problems per day over time because the problems increase in difficulty. Note that the end date is June 5th and not June 4th because there are 64 days in the first circle which is one day over nine weeks. Note that there are 1209 problems in CT-ART 3.0 – that is why the Total Completed column shows that I have completed 1209.

You should stick to this schedule even if you are on vacation or playing in a tournament. Constant drilling is absolutely essential.

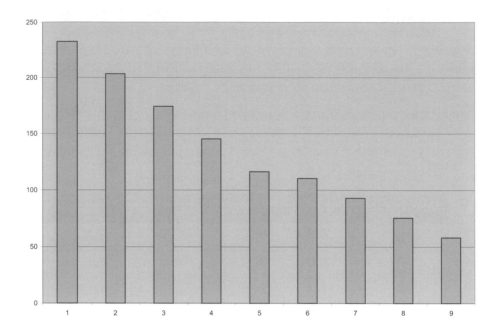

*Figure 19: Number of tactical problems per week during the first cycle of the seven cycles. Notice that the number falls drastically – the number of problems done in the last week is approximately one-fifth of the problems done in the first week – because the problems are ordered by difficulty.*

In the 64-day circle spend no more than five minutes trying to find the first move and no more than an additional five minutes working through the solution. If you fail to solve the problem within the allotted five minutes, simply use the second five-minute time slot to read and study the solution. When you are working through the initial problems in your 1000 problem set, you should find the first move in much less than five minutes. If you are not, then the problems are too difficult. In my 64-day circle I did not use the full ten-minute time period with any frequency until the last four weeks when the number of problems I solved per day was relatively small.

My 32-day circle schedule is shown in Figure 20 and the number of problems per week is shown graphically in Figure 21.

My schedule for the third circle is shown in Figure 22 and the number of problems I did per week is shown in graphical form in Figure 23.

| | Per week | Per day | Total Completed | End date |
|---|---|---|---|---|
| 1 | 436 | 62.3 | 436 | Jun 11th |
| 2 | 320 | 45.7 | 756 | Jun 18th |
| 3 | 227 | 32.4 | 983 | Jun 25th |
| 4 | 168 | 24.0 | 1151 | Jul 2nd |
| 5 | 58 | 8.3 | 1209 | Jul 6th |

*Figure 20: My schedule for the second week of the Seven Circles program. Note that I chose to do the same number of problems in the final week as I did in the final week in the first circle. There were two reasons for this: First, it was a short week (only four days) and, second, I planned to be playing in a tournament on July 4th.*

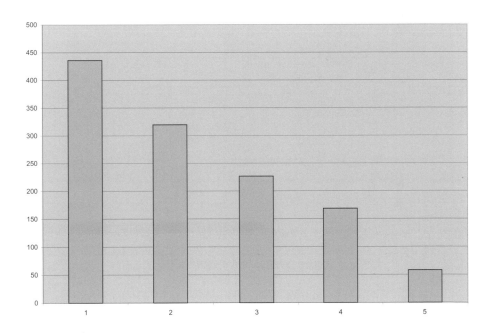

*Figure 21: Number of problems per week during the second circle. Note that in the fifth week the number of problems I completed was about one-seventh of the number of problems I did during the first week. Make sure to allow for a steep drop off so that you have the time to solve the hardest problems. If you try to cram too many of the hard problems over a short period of time, then you will become tired and frustrated and will lose the discipline required to stay with the schedule.*

|   | Per week | Per day | Total completed | End date |
|---|----------|---------|-----------------|----------|
| 1 | 756 | 108.0 | 756 | Jul 13th |
| 2 | 395 | 56.4 | 1151 | Jul 20th |
| 3 | 58 | 8.0 | 1209 | Jul 22nd |

*Figure 22: Schedule for the third circle in the Seven Circles.*

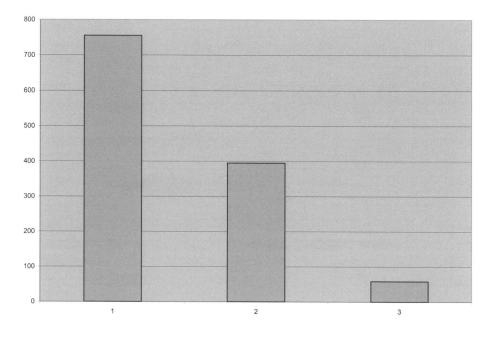

*Figure 23: Number of problems per week in the third circle. Again I kept the number of problems that I did in the last week constant. Note, however, that in the third circle the third week is only two days.*

For the last four circles I went from a weekly schedule to a daily schedule. The weekly schedule does allow for some flexibility. If I am feeling particularly well rested and mentally alert on some day – or if the problems are particularly easy – then I can do more than my quota, thus giving me a cushion for a day when I am not feeling so chipper.

A daily schedule, however, leaves almost no room for error. You must make sure at the start of the Seven Circles that you will have fifteen days with no distraction available to complete the last four circles. If you do not, I suggest that you continue doing chess vision exercises until you are sure that you will be able to complete the Seven Circles in one contiguous 127-day period. Seven Circles loses much of its strength if it is not completed in one gulp.

My daily schedule for the fourth circle is shown in Figure 24 and the number of problems I did per day is shown graphically in Figure 25.

|   | Per day | Total completed | End date |
|---|---------|-----------------|----------|
| 1 | 400 | 400 | Jul 23rd |
| 2 | 301 | 701 | Jul 24thl |
| 3 | 188 | 889 | Jul 25th |
| 4 | 126 | 1015 | Jul 26th |
| 5 | 84 | 1099 | Jul 27th |
| 6 | 55 | 1154 | Jul 28th |
| 7 | 35 | 1189 | Jul 29th |
| 8 | 20 | 1209 | Jul 30th |

*Figure 24: Schedule for the fourth circle*

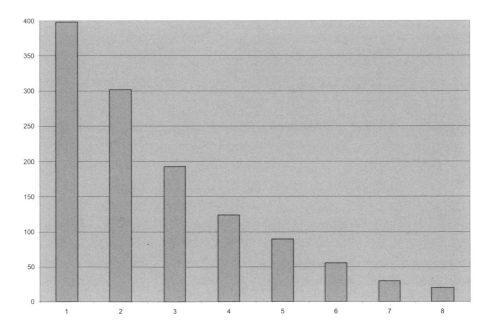

*Figure 25: Number of problems per day during the fourth circle.*

For the fifth circle, the schedule is shown in Figure 26 and the number of problems per day is shown in Figure 27.

| | Per day | Total completed | End date |
|---|---|---|---|
| 1 | 470 | 470 | Jul 31st |
| 2 | 379 | 849 | Aug 1st |
| 3 | 225 | 1074 | Aug 2nd |
| 4 | 135 | 1209 | Aug 3rd |

*Figure 26: Schedule for the fifth circle.*

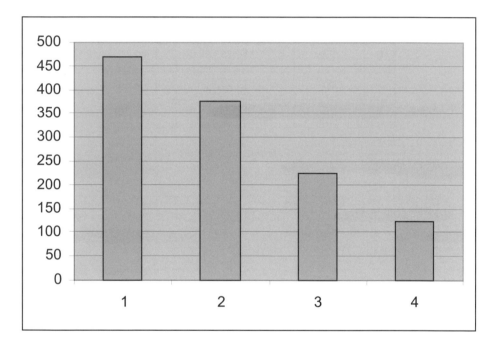

*Figure 27: Number of problems per day during the fifth circle.*

For the sixth circle, the schedule I followed is shown Figure 28. Because so many problems are done every day, making sure that you are working hard on every problem is critical. You should simply remember the solutions to many of the problems, but if you do not, put your best effort into finding the solution in the short time that is given. Avoid at all costs a defeatist mentality in which you wait for the time to be up so that you can move onto the next problem.

| | Per day | Total completed | End date |
|---|---|---|---|
| 1 | 809 | 809 | Aug 4th |
| 2 | 400 | 1209 | Aug 5th |

*Figure 28: Number of problems per day in the sixth circle.*

For the seventh circle, I did, of course, all 1209 problems in one day, giving myself five to ten minutes of rest every hour.

And on the 128th day I rested.

## Summary

The purpose of the Seven Circles program is to drill a set of 1000 positions into your brain. During the first four circles you will focus on your calculation ability and during the last three you will focus on your recognition ability. You do not need to put any special effort into focusing on calculation or recognition. The process itself – the constant repetition combined with the reduction in time allowed per problem – will force you to move to recognising patterns instead of calculating combinations.

Both of these abilities – calculation and recognition – are critical. During games you have to very quickly, often within two minutes, recognise that there is a tactical opportunity.

What should you do after the Seven Circles? Continue to work on tactical problems on a daily basis. If If you feel that you need additional work, choose another 1000 problems and go through them using the Seven Circles technique.

# Chapter Three

# How to Think

During the third and final step of this program, you will learn how to incorporate your newly developed tactical skills in your over-the-board (OTB) play.

When I first developed this study program there was no third step. I thought that the first two steps would be enough. Unfortunately, I soon discovered that transferring my tactical ability to OTB games was quite difficult. Repeatedly I would look at the board for a few seconds, decide that there was no tactical shot and then make what I thought was a reasonable move. Time and time again I would turn out to be wrong and lose my queen or allow a mate.

As a result, I decided that I needed to develop a more structured way to think about my moves during the game. I experimented with several recipes and finally arrived at an eight-step procedure. Immediately after my opponent makes a move I do the following (the time for each step and the total time spent are noted after each step):

1) Make a physical movement. Initially I shuffled my legs but found that they got tired in long games. Now I shift around in my chair, move my arms up and down, or wiggle my toes (5 seconds; total time: 5 seconds).

2) Look at the board with Chess Vision, the ability developed by going through the micro-level drills described in a previous chapter (10 seconds; total time: 15 seconds).

3) Understand what the opponent is threatening (20 seconds; total time: 35 seconds).

4) Write down the opponent's move on my score sheet (5 seconds; total time: 40 seconds).

5) If the opponent has a serious threat, then respond. If not, calculate a tactical sequence. If no tactical sequence exists, implement a plan (70 seconds; total time: 110 seconds).

6) Write down my move (5 seconds; total time: 115 seconds).

7) Imagine the position after I make my intended move and use Chess Vision to check the position. If Chess Vision does not locate any problems, make the move and press the clock. If Chess Vision does locate a problem, go back to step 1. (10 seconds; total time: 125 seconds).

8) Make sure that I have pressed the clock.

Step 5's 'implement a plan' is the only step that is not self-explanatory. I implement very simple plans (as opposed to Silman, Kotov and Pachman-like plans) that improvo tho probability that thoro will bo a tactical shot. These plans include:

1) Improve the mobility of the pieces.

2) Prevent the opponent from castling.

3) Trade off pawns.

4) Keep the queen on the board.

I force myself to implement these plans very quickly. No 'long thinks' are allowed. I very rarely spend more than five minutes on a position and, as a result, win approximately 10% of my games because my opponent gets into time trouble. At the class level, spending time creating a complicated plan is often counterproductive. While you are executing a longwinded plan you or your opponent will almost certainly make a tactical error which will drastically change the evaluation of the plan.

Note that this approach is sharply different from Kotov's thinking technique, which is probably the best known move selection method. In *Think like a Grandmaster*, Kotov writes: 'All candidate moves should be identified at once and listed in one's head.' This advice is, of course, simply ridiculous for the class player. Unless a specific algorithm is given for identifying the candidate moves this is equivalent to saying: 'If there is a five-move combination that wins, make the five-move combination.' I can imagine a post-mortem conversation between Kotov and a class player:

Class player: Here I played ♖a7.

Kotov: You should not have played that move.

Class player: Why?

Kotov: It is not a candidate move.

Show me a class player who can follow Kotov's thinking technique and achieve success and I'll show you a Master masquerading as a patzer.

After Kotov's thinking technique, possibly the second best known approach to selecting moves based on positional considerations is the Silman thinking technique as discussed in *Reassess Your Chess.* Silman's technique, which is based on imbalances, may be useful for the class player but only if you place tactical considerations ahead of positional considerations.

Following this eight-step sequence on every move, including opening moves and positions where you have a mate in one, is absolutely critical. The requirement of going through this sequence on every move means that you cannot play blitz. The main problem with blitz is that it interferes with the mental discipline required to succeed at long time controls. After you have worked through the five-month program and have spent many months using the eight-step sequence in OTB play and your rating has improved several hundred points, then you can play blitz.

The eight-step process described above is what I do after my opponent makes a move. I do not have a formal process I go through after I make my move and am waiting for my opponent to move. However, I do know that sitting at the table and looking at the position is critical to my success. If I get up and walk around, my effective rating declines by at least 100 points. So stay in your chair and think about the game instead of getting up and wandering around the room, looking at your friend's games. See Figure 29 for an example of the focus that you should bring to your games.

*The only time that you should leave the game is if you absolutely must go to the restroom.* In these cases follow National Master Larry Tamarkin's rule: 'Tamarkin's rule about returning from the bathroom: sit down, take a stress pill and think things over!' This is particularly true if you are thinking of doing something bold, such as sacrificing a queen for mate.

*Figure 29: Author Michael de la Maza (immediate right) focuses on the board and only on the board during the 2001 World Open. Michael finished in first place in the U2000 section and won $10,000*

# Sample Game

In this section, I show how I thought through one particular game using the process I describe above. The process is tedious – in the opening there are rarely significant threats and in this particular game there are no significant tactical opportunities until the end of the game.

But you must force yourself to work through the entire eight-step process on every move; otherwise you will develop poor habits and miss tactical opportunities when they arise. After you have gained hundreds of points and are no longer a class player, then you can begin to take short cuts.

I am White in this game and my opponent is a rapidly improving Class A player.

Opponent's threat (step 2/3): No significant threats.
Decide move (step 5): 1 e4 of course!

**1 e4 c5**

Opponent's threat (step 2/3): No significant threats, but watch out for ...♛a5.
Decide move (step 5): No tactics. 2 ♘f3 or 2 ♘c3 are both reasonable.

**2 ♘f3 d6**

Opponent's threat (step 2/3): No significant threats.
Decide move (step 5): No tactics. 3 e5 is most shocking. Continue development with 3 ♘c3.

**3 ♘c3 ♘f6**

Opponent's threat (step 2/3): No significant threats.
Decide move (step 5): No tactics. Continue to develop with 4 ♗b5+.

**4 ♗b5+ ♗d7**

Opponent's threat (step 2/3): No significant threats but light-squared bishop is attacked.
Decide move (step 5): No tactics.

**5 ♗xd7+ ♕xd7**

Opponent's threat (step 2/3): No significant threats.
Decide move (step 5): No tactics. 6 e5 continues to be quite interesting, at least in part because it creates a crazy position that Black will not know: 6...dxe5 7 ♘xe5 ♕e6 8 f4. Stay safe with 6 0-0.

**6 0-0 ♘c6**

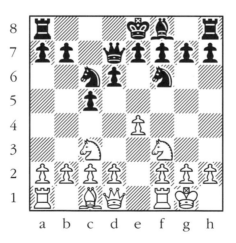

Opponent's threat (step 2/3): ...♘d4 is unpleasant.
Decide move (step 5): No tactics. Exchange pawns and open up centre with 7 d4.

**7 d4 cxd4**

Opponent's threat (step 2/3): Threatening ...dxc3
Decide move (step 5): Tactics – must recapture.

**8 ♘xd4 e6**

Opponent's threat (step 2/3): No significant threats, but must watch for ...♘xd4.
Decide move (step 5): No tactics. Develop piece and attempt to disrupt pawn structure with ♗g5.

**9 ♗g5 ♗e7**

Opponent's threat (step 2/3): g5-bishop is unprotected and must be monitored. Fortunately ...♘xe4 does not work because after ...♘xe4 the e4-knight protects the g5-bishop.
Decide move (step 5): No tactics. Connect rooks with ♕d3, but must watch for ...♘b4.

**10 ♕d3 0-0**

Opponent's threat (step 2/3): g5-bishop still unprotected.
Decide move (step 5): No tactics. Which rook to which square? 11 ♖ad1 supports queen and adds pressure down open file.

**11 ♖ad1 a6**

Opponent's threat (step 2/3): g5-bishop unprotected.
Decide move (step 5): Opportunity for tactics starting with 12 ♘xc6 – either disrupt pawn structure or win pawn.

**12 ♘xc6 bxc6**

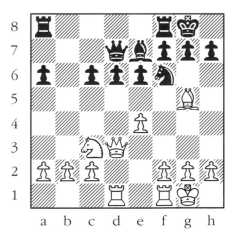

Opponent's threat (step 2/3): g5-bishop unprotected.
Decide move (step 5): Opportunity for tactics. Black must either lose d-pawn or expose king.

**13 ♗xf6 gxf6**

Opponent's threat (step 2/3): No significant threats.
Decide move (step 5): No tactics. Move pieces to attack king. White has the advantage.

**14 ♘e2 ♛b7**

Opponent's threat (step 2/3): ...♛xb2
Decide move (step 5): Tactics – must protect pawn.

**15 b3 d5**

Opponent's threat (step 2/3): Black has a strong centre pawn mass.
Decide move (step 5): No tactics. 16 exd5 strengthens black's pawn centre.

**16 c4 ♜fd8**

Opponent's threat (step 2/3): Queen is exposed down d-file.
Decide move (step 5): No tactics. Remove queen with tempo.

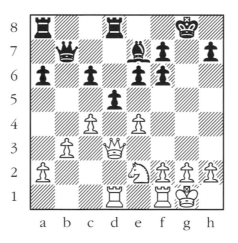

**17 ♛g3+ ♚h8**

Opponent's threat (step 2/3): No threats.
Decide move (step 5): No tactics. Liquidate pawns.

**18 cxd5 cxd5**

Opponent's threat (step 2/3): No threats.
Decide move (step 5): No tactics. Liquidate pawns.

**19 exd5 ♖xd5**

Opponent's threat (step 2/3): No threats.
Decide move (step 5): No tactics. Attempt to keep pieces on board.

**20 ♕f3 ♖ad8**

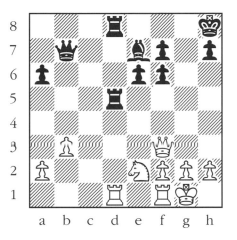

Opponent's threat (step 2/3): 21...♖xd1 22 ♕xb7? ♖xf1+ 23 ♔xf1 ♖d1 mate.
Decide move (step 5): Protect rook.

**21 ♘c3 ♖5d7**

Opponent's threat (step 2/3): ...♖xd1 is still problematic.
Decide move (step 5): No tactics. Liquidate to endgame. White's advantage is gone.

**22 ♕xb7 ♖xb7**

Opponent's threat (step 2/3): No threats.
Decide move (step 5): No tactics. Continue to liquidate.

**23 ♖xd8+ ♗xd8**

Opponent's threat (step 2/3): No threats.
Decide move (step 5): No tactics. Control open file.

**24 ♖d1 ♗e7**

Opponent's threat (step 2/3): No threats.

Decide move (step 5): No tactics. Centralise king.

**25 ♔f1 ♖c7**

Opponent's threat (step 2/3): ...♖xc3.
Decide move (step 5): Protect knight. Knight has been used very poorly during the game.

**26 ♘e2 ♖c2**

Opponent's threat (step 2/3): Black's rook has penetrated white's position. Immediate threat is ...♖xa2.
Decide move (step 5): Protect pawn.

**27 a4 ♖b2**

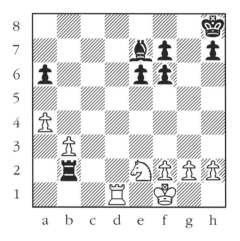

Opponent's threat (step 2/3): ...♖xb3
Decide move (step 5): Prepare for rook penetration. Both sides can draw by simply sacrificing minor piece for last pawn.

**28 ♘f4 ♖xb3**

Opponent's threat (step 2/3): ...♖b4 forking a pawn and f4-knight.
Decide move (step 5): Penetrate with rook.

**29 ♖d7 ♖b1+**

Opponent's threat (step 2/3): ♖b4.
Decide move (step 5): Forced move.

**30 ♔e2 ♖b2+**

Opponent's threat (step 2/3): Trap king on kingside.
Decide move (step 5): Activate king.

**31 ♔f3 ♜b3+**

Opponent's threat (step 2/3): Trap king on kingside.
Decide move (step 5): Activate king.

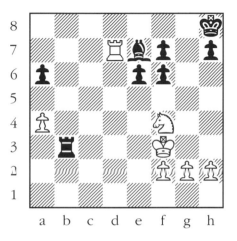

**32 ♔g4 f5+**

Opponent's threat (step 2/3): ...♜b4
Decide move (step 5): Opportunity to mate or win material.

**33 ♔h5 ♜b4**

Opponent's threat (step 2/3): ...♜xf4.
Decide move (step 5): Protect knight. Exchanging minor pieces loses on the spot.

**34 g3 ♝f8**

Opponent's threat (step 2/3): No threats.
Decide move (step 5): Win material.

**35 ♜xf7 ♔g8**

Opponent's threat (step 2/3): ...♝xf7.
Decide move (step 5): Remove rook and attack pawn.

**36 ♜a7 ♜b6**

Opponent's threat (step 2/3): ...♜xa4 is not a threat. It loses to ♘xe6.

Decide move (step 5): Activate king.

**37 ♔g5 ♗c5**

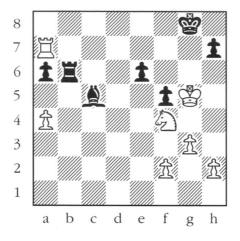

Opponent's threat (step 2/3): f-, g- and h-pawns are all on dark squares.
Decide move (step 5): Prepare to defend.

**38 ♖d7 ♗xf2**

Opponent's threat (step 2/3): No threats.
Decide move (step 5): Threaten mate.

**39 ♔f6 ♖b8**

Opponent's threat (step 2/3): No threats.
Decide move (step 5): Win material.

**40 ♘xe6 ♗g1**

Opponent's threat (step 2/3): ...♗xh2.
Decide move (step 5): Protect h-pawn.

**41 h3 ♗e3**

Opponent's threat (step 2/3): No threats.
Decide move (step 5): Win material. White is now winning.

**42 ♔xf5 ♖a8**

Opponent's threat (step 2/3): No threats.
Decide move (step 5): Attack and threaten ♘c7.

**43 ♖d6 ♗c1**

Opponent's threat (step 2/3): No threats.
Decide move (step 5): Fix a pawn.

**44 a5 ♗a3**

Opponent's threat (step 2/3): ...♗xd6
Decide move (step 5): Protect rook.

**45 ♖b6 ♖a7**

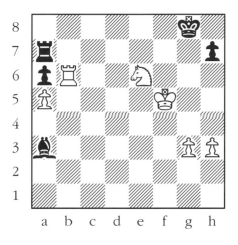

Opponent's threat (step 2/3): No threats.
Decide move (step 5): The game is over. ♖b8-♖h8.

**46 ♖b8+ ♔f7**

Opponent's threat (step 2/3): No threats.
Decide move (step 5): Skewer rook.

**47 ♖h8 Black resigns**

Although thinking like this throughout a game at this level of detail may seem boring and useless, I encourage you to adopt this policy for at least 200 games. During practice games you may even consider writing down your thoughts as you move through the eight-step process so that you are sure you have not missed a step. Alternatively, you might also consider using a tape recorder during practice games. This will speed up the process and allow you to focus on the game itself. However, you must be sure to then transcribe your thoughts and analyse them.

## Post-mortem

After every game you should analyse it with a chess program and produce charts such as those shown in Figure 30 and Figure 31. These graphs show how the computer program evaluates the position after every white move during the course of the game.

With one quick glance at Figure 30 you can see that White had a significant advantage early in the game shown above which he then frittered away and had to regain in the endgame. You can also see that Black made a 1.5 pawn error on move 45.

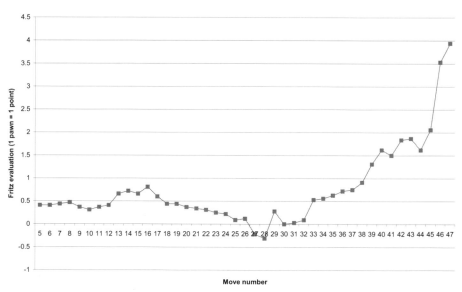

Figure 30: Evaluation graph for the sample game. After every move, the score that Fritz gives is written down and then graphed. Positive scores mean that White has the advantage and negative scores mean that Black has the advantage. In this game White had the advantage, lost it, and then regained it.

Looking at Figure 31, White should concentrate on moves 16 to 28, during which he lost over one point. After 16 c4, the position is shown in the diagram below, as is the position after 28 ♘f4. White should also examine move 30, which appears to have lost approximately a quarter of a point.

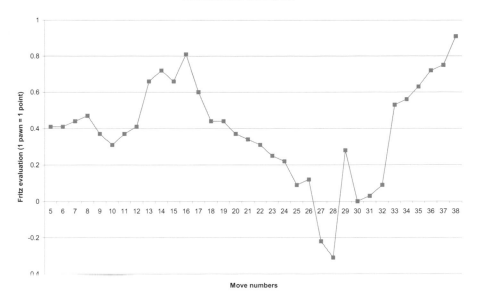

Evaluation after white moves

*Figure 31: A detail of the evaluation graph. When the evaluation changes sharply (which usually happens at the end of the game when one player starts to clearly win) it is often helpful to graph just a section of the game to see it in greater detail. This graph shows that around move fifteen White had an almost won game but then suffered a reversal greater than one pawn over the next dozen moves and was actually at a disadvantage at the beginning of the endgame.*

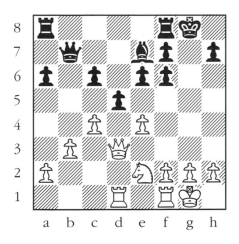

*Position after 16 c4. This is the high point of White's game until move 38.*

Conversely, Black should concentrate on what happened during the six move sequence between move 28 and move 33, during which Black went from having a slight advantage to being at a significant disadvantage.

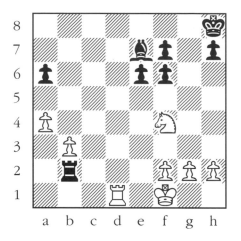

*Position after 28 ♘f4. The low point for White over the course of the game.*

Comparing the two diagrams above, there are two facts that immediately jump out. First, the game has moved from a middlegame position to an endgame position. Second, Black's weak king position, which White had worked so hard to produce, cannot be easily exploited in the second diagram.

Note that this post-mortem analysis did not involve detailed variations, opening analysis or a careful examination of every move. Instead the entire focus was on achieving a simple, yet useful, understanding of how White lost his advantage.

How does this simple analysis help White during future games? Remember that in step 5 of the eight-step sequence described earlier in this chapter, you are to implement a simple plan if there are no threats or tactical opportunities.

What this game suggests is that the tactical player should attempt to keep pieces on the board until a significant advantage is attained. During the game White consciously attempted to trade down and thus lost his advantage. Instead of simplifying, White should focus on complicating the position until he has a material advantage. In this game White succeeded in exposing the black king, but then traded off the queen and a rook, making it difficult to mount a direct attack.

This type of simple analysis can be completed for any game in approximately half an hour. Start by processing the game using Fritz or another computer program and then focus on the move sequences that cause the greatest change.

Move sequences that result in a change of qualitative evaluation (e.g., White has a significant advantage at the beginning of the sequence and Black has a slight advantage at the end of the sequence) are of the most interest.

Once you have identified these sequences, simply look at the positions and try to ascertain how the advantage was lost or gained and adjust your understanding of the game to reduce the probability that this will happen again.

Note that I did not spend time analysing single positions and working out many variations. At the class level, there is no need to do so and relatively little benefit from putting so much effort into a single game. Instead, understand how you erred in constructing your simple plans and then move on to study more tactics.

In this game there were no significant tactical errors by either side until the very end of the game. This is quite unusual. Usually class games feature multiple tactical errors by both sides. A more typical example is shown in Figure 32. In this game I was playing Black and made a significant tactical error in the opening but succeeded in clawing back only to be down a pawn in a rook and pawn ond game. Fortunately, White was not able to pull through and the game was drawn.

Looking at the graph makes clear what White and Black need to focus on. Black should correct the opening error and White should work on closing out games.

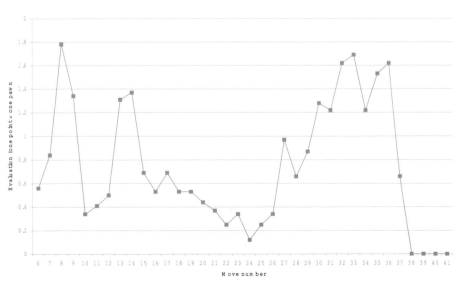

Figure 32: A typical game between class players features
*significant swings due to tactical errors.*

If the computer analysis identifies that you have made a tactical error, spend time to create a chess vision drill around that particular error and study other tactical problems that are similar to the one that arose in the game.

## Summary

Once you have followed the advice in this book, drilled chess vision problems and run through the Seven Circles, you need to make sure that you apply this tactical ability during the game.

After I finished Seven Circles I regularly found myself taking a glance at the board, deciding that there were no tactical opportunities, and then making a move. When analysing the game with Fritz, I found that I missed many tactical shots so I decided to structure my thinking process on every move.

The specific steps that you follow when making a move are not all that important. What is important is that you have a method that forces you to think tactically on every move. In order to develop good habits, avoid playing blitz until you have played many games at slow time controls that allow you to execute your thinking algorithm.

# Chapter Four

# Practical Tactics

In this chapter I show tactics from games between class players to give you an illustration of how well you will have to perform at various levels of play.

These tactical problems differ from those that appear in other sources in three ways. First, all of the tactical sequences were played by class players while they were class players. The vast majority of tactical puzzles drawn from real games are from master level players. As a result, understanding exactly how refined your tactical ability must be in order to excel at the class level is difficult. Second, all of the games are drawn from actual games played under tournament conditions. Many tactical problems are composed, again making understanding how tactically strong you need to be at the class level more difficult to estimate. Third, in the problems given below the position is often lopsided at the start of the tactical sequence as often happens in class games but is rare in standard tactical puzzles. As such, the tactical sequences often serve to finish a won game quickly; a very valuable ability during weekend tournaments when conserving energy is critical.

Remember that these problems were played under tournament conditions so it is unlikely that any tactical sequence took more than three minutes to calculate. If you want to test yourself, you should allow no more than two minutes per sequence. Solutions are at the back of the book.

# Tactics from Games where players are between 1200 USCF and 1600 USCF

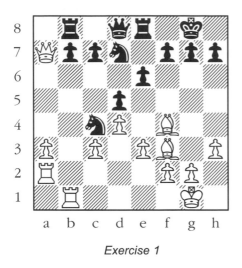

Exercise 1

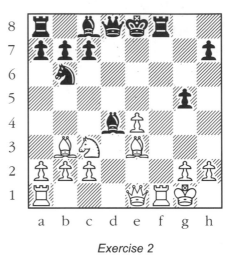

Exercise 2

**Exercise 1:** Black to play and win.

**Exercise 2:** White to play and win.

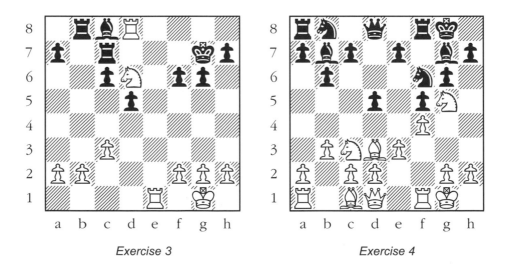

Exercise 3

Exercise 4

**Exercise 3:** White to play and win.

**Exercise 4:** White to play and win.

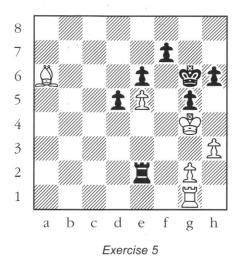

Exercise 5

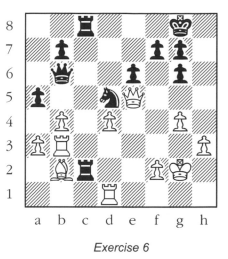

Exercise 6

**Exercise 5:** Black to play and mate.

**Exercise 6:** Black to play and win.

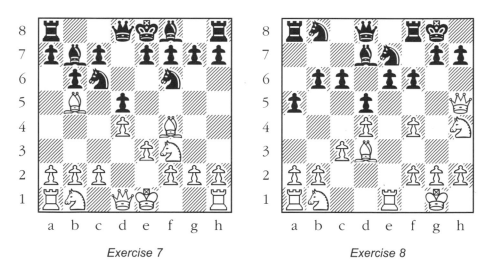

Exercise 7

Exercise 8

**Exercise 7:** White to play and win.

**Exercise 8:** White to play and mate.

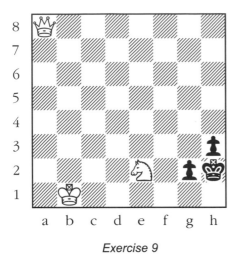

*Exercise 9*

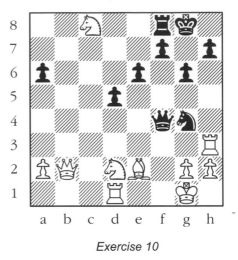

*Exercise 10*

**Exercise 9:** White to play and mate

**Exercise 10:** White to play and win

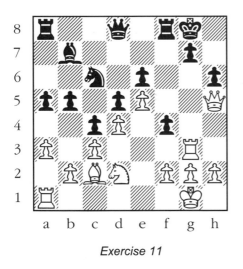

*Exercise 11*

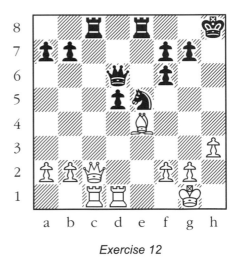

*Exercise 12*

**Exercise 11:** White to play and win.

**Exercise 12:** White to play and win.

# Tactics from games in which both players are between USCF 1400 and USCF 1800

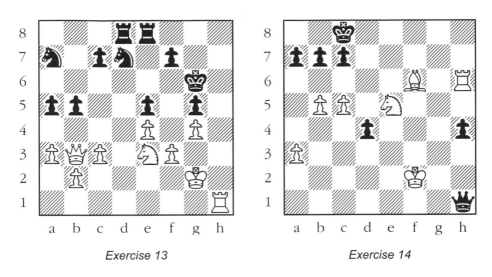

Exercise 13                      Exercise 14

**Exercise 13:** White to play and mate.

**Exercise 14:** Black to play and finish off the game.

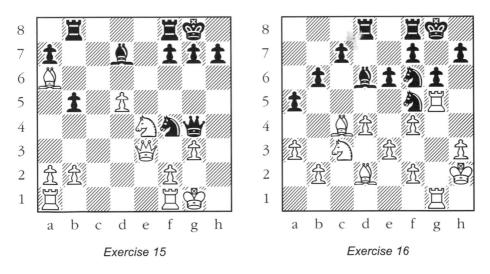

Exercise 15                      Exercise 16

**Exercise 15:** Black to play and finish off the game.

**Exercise 16:** Black to play and win.

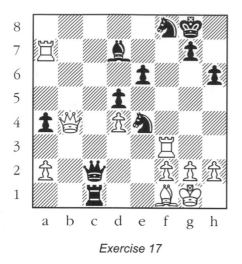

*Exercise 17*

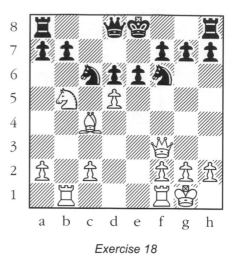

*Exercise 18*

**Exercise 17:** Black to play and mate.

**Exercise 18:** Black to play and win.

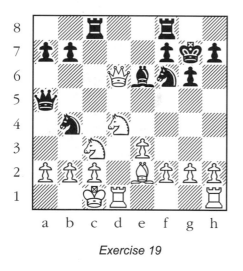

*Exercise 19*

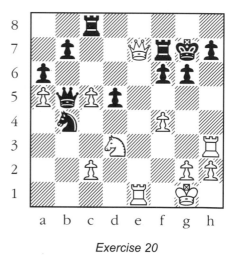

*Exercise 20*

**Exercise 19:** Black to play and win.

**Exercise 20:** White to play and win.

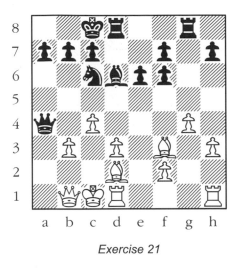

*Exercise 21*

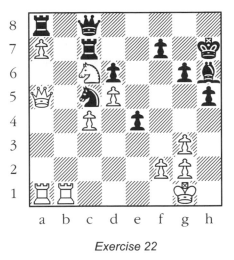

*Exercise 22*

**Exercise 21:** Black to play and win

**Exercise 22:** White to play and win.

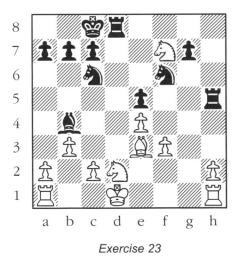

*Exercise 23*

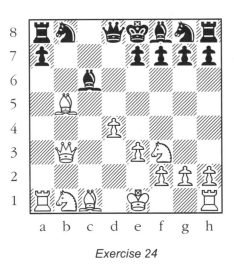

*Exercise 24*

**Exercise 23:** Black to play and win.

**Exercise 24:** White to play and win.

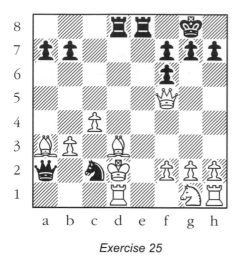

*Exercise 25*

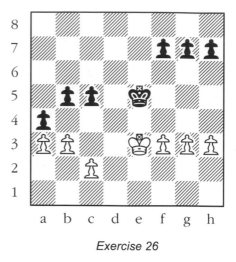

*Exercise 26*

**Exercise 25:** Black to play and win.

**Exercise 26:** Black to play and win.

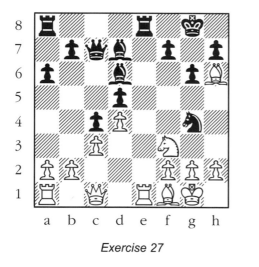

*Exercise 27*

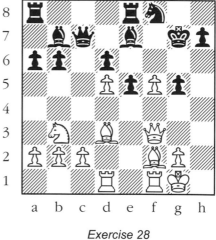

*Exercise 28*

**Exercise 27:** Black to play and mate.

**Exercise 28:** White to move and win.

# Tactics from games in which both players are between USCF 1600 and USCF 2000

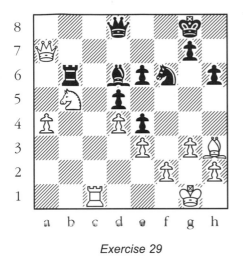

*Exercise 29*

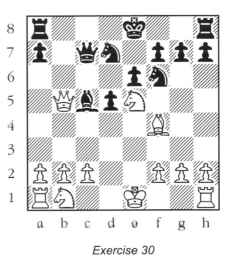

*Exercise 30*

**Exercise 29:** White to play and win.

**Exercise 30:** Black to play and win.

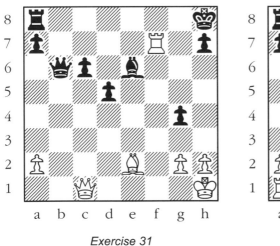

*Exercise 31*

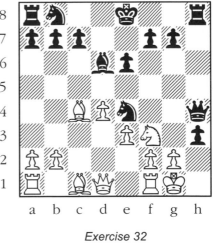

*Exercise 32*

**Exercise 31:** White to play and win.

**Exercise 32:** Black to play and win.

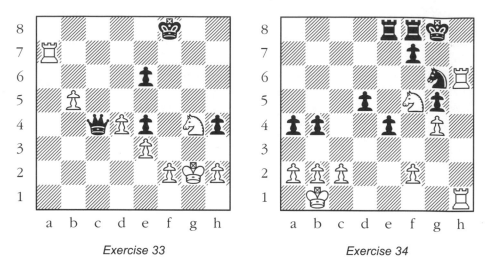

Exercise 33

Exercise 34

**Exercise 33:** White to play and win.

**Exercise 34:** White to move and mate.

The following eight positions are all from the 2001 World Open where I finished clear first in the Under 2000 section and won $10,000 for my efforts.

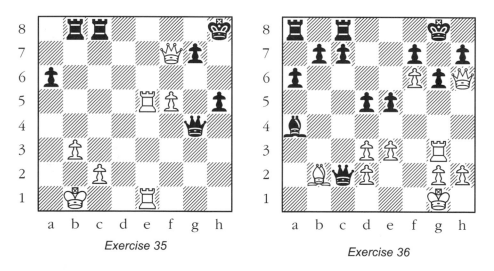

Exercise 35

Exercise 36

**Exercise 35:** Material is equal, but White has a big attack. Where is the win?

**Exercise 36:** In my second game, White was one move away from mate. However, Black has a sequence which gets in first. What is it?

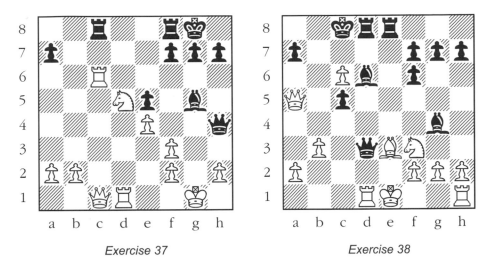

Exercise 37

Exercise 38

**Exercise 37:** In the third game my opponent made too much of my fractured pawn structure and too little of my great knight. How does White win?

**Exercise 38:** In the fourth game, both players are gunning for the opposing king. However, it is Black's move and he gets in first. How?

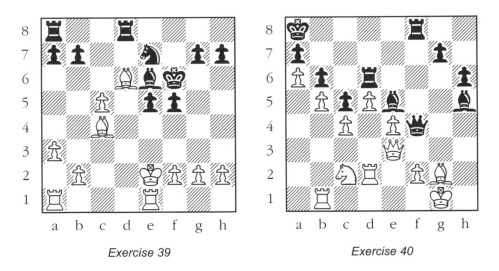

Exercise 39

Exercise 40

**Exercise 39:** In the fifth game I was a pawn down but got lucky. How does White now win?

**Exercise 40:** The seventh game saw a tactically difficult middlegame but then my opponent made a simple mistake right after the time control. Black to play.

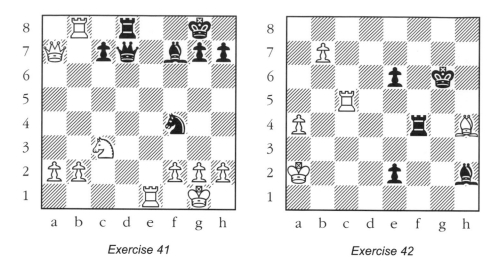

*Exercise 41*          *Exercise 42*

**Exercise 41:** In the eighth game my opponent decided to push on in a completely lost position: how does White now win?

**Exercise 42:** The ninth game was the psychologically most difficult game of my life. I was clearly lost but my opponent missed a simple winning shot on two successive moves. He finally blundered the game away. How does White now win?

# Chapter Five

# Success with Rapid Chess Improvement

Since the first half of 2000, thousands of chess players have learned about chess vision drills and the Seven Circles chess improvement techniques and dozens have written to me about their experiences.

In this chapter I share with you some of the experiences of these players. Some have adapted the program to suit their needs, some have supplemented the program with their own study lines, and some have simply followed the program straight through. All have seen their chess abilities improve by following the tenets of the Rapid Chess Improvement program.

Use the stories of these chess players to inspire you to complete the chess training program described in this book. It does work! If you start and find the going slow or difficult, reread this section to fire up your ambition.

## The story of Cuzear Ford: Becoming a Class B player

Cuzear Ford was a long time Class C chess player (see Figure 33) when he came across the Rapid Chess Improvement study program.

After implementing just part of the program, his rating shot up immediately to the Class B level. His rating jumped 122 points in just one two month period. As a point of comparison, my rating never increased more than 100 points over any two-month period even though I, like Cuzear, started at the Class D level. Cuzear's success with the program proves that my experience is not unique. The Rapid Chess Improvement method can be learned and applied by just about anyone. The results come quickly and the performance gains are significant.

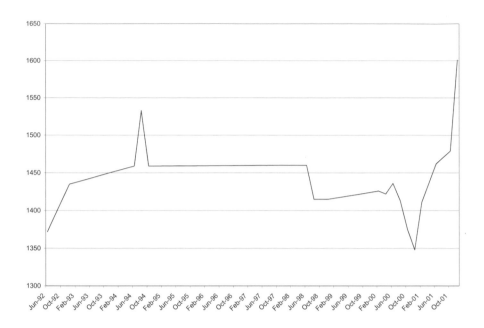

*Figure 33: Cuzear Ford's chess rating. Cuzear was a Class D/Class C player for over eight years when he discovered the Rapid Chess Improvement study plan. His rating shot up to the Class B level almost immediately.*

Shortly after I began to discuss the key concepts in the Rapid Chess Improvement program Cuzear wrote to tell me: 'You have given me confidence to stay on course and pursue some of your insights further.'

After he had studied the ideas and concepts further he wrote me a very thoughtful email (I lightly edited the email to make it more readable, but it still contains Cuzear's uniquely expressed enthusiasm):

'I admit, when I first read how you improve (Seven Circles) I thought ... people would not do the Seven Circles because it appeared to be too difficult and many would have a problem with their level of consistency in completing the Seven Circles. ... The point is you have discovered a concrete method of rapid chess development. Period! It doesn't matter who likes it or who thinks it's too hard. The program is within their reach because you started this as a D player and it thus demonstrated its power. There was nothing to suggest that when you started Seven Circles that you had some special talent or that you were a promising D player on the rise. Quite the contrary I suspect.

Your method is pure genius. Here is why.

First! Simplicity – by studying tactics (Seven Circles method) you will achieve rapid chess development. Now let's weigh in on this. Most people will agree that if they want to improve they must study tactics. No big deal. The truth is studying tactics often has equal billing with studying strategic ideas. So they try to learn both. Or they may put more time into learning strategic ideas (because they may be more entertaining) at the expense of rapid tactics training. Contrary, you put all emphasis on studying tactics, reasoning that a chess player is learning concrete winning methods. Most aspiring chess players really don't appreciate that learning tactics is a fundamental that should be mastered. Therefore the fundamental is not basic knowledge of tactics but an ongoing desire to achieve exceptional knowledge. So the fundamental becomes exceptional not basic knowledge. Your program accelerates that process. Imagine if every chess coach communicated to their eager students that the only way to achieve rapid results or any kind of results at all is through the method rapid tactics training. I believe now that rapid tactics training should be a fundamental teaching tool for trainers. Any teacher who doesn't teach as such isn't worth much. It is like a golf coach who doesn't take advantage of the modern use of video equipment when analysing a student's golf swing. You have convinced me that strong chess tactics is a fundamental that should be over-emphasised over strategic concepts.

Second, the special class of adult chess players can relate to your story. You are one of us. Therefore, your story has credibility and makes us believe that if we do as you do we too can experience rapid chess development. Or at least improve faster than we would otherwise.

Third, the program is doable in a very short period of time. That is exciting.

Fourth, the knowledge is concrete, which makes it useful immediately. A strong tactical player doesn't need to understand the strategic value of a rook on the open file. He will not only naturally understand its strategic value, but will creatively exploit his advantage. That's what tactics do for you – it forces you to think creatively.

I could go on and on. Keep this in mind. This program isn't for everyone. It is for people like you and I who are serious about chess improvement. *People who are tired of messing around, losing games, having less fun. It is for people who aren't lazy. The best aspect of this program is that you have provided a vehicle for people such as myself to rapidly increase my strength and to maintain my independence away from high-priced coaches.*

Whether the program is fun or not is not important to me anymore. What matters is... If I do this, I get that (something concrete).

The reward will be the steady climb in my chess club and the amazement of my peers. Man, I just can't wait. Thank you so much, you've done good for a lot of people.'

This email message is typical of those that I have received from people who have really thought through the method. They realise that as adult class players they have two choices: They can continue to make three move tactical errors and stay at the class player level or they can work through the Rapid Chess Improvement program and see huge increases in their playing ability.

As Cuzear says, however, the program is not for people who are lazy. Chess is hard and it takes hard work to get better. The Rapid Chess Improvement program will teach you the fastest, most time effective way to improve, but you will still have to put in hundreds of hours of hard work.

At another time Cuzear wrote:

'I have yet to miss a day in the Seven Circles program. I can see already how it is going to help. So many of my chess club friends aren't doing anything close to this, nor do they care too. They all say they want to improve significantly, but somehow refuse to see the error of their ways. Some just don't know what to do, so many others are comfortable and still enjoy the game where they are. The rest some have legitimate life commitments to family, work etc. that interfere with consistent chess work. I guess we all have to cope with life vicissitudes, but some more than others.

I breezed through the first 225 or so puzzles and that was only because I've studied many of the checkmating patterns such as Morphy's mate, Pillsbury's mate, Greco's mate, Anastasia's, Arabian mate, Philidor's smothered mate; I think you get the point (smile). One night I completed 60 puzzles at a 91% rate. Overall I am at 87%, and of course I learned from the ones I missed. Now I'm stuck. And I'm a little concerned that I'm stuck so early in the program. For the remaining problems I must calculate in a more precise way without the help of some obvious patterns. *I guess I underestimated what intermediate tactics was all about. I thought the tough stuff would come much later for me.* I can't imagine what puzzle 1000 will look like. It seems I have a long way to go. One problem is I can only do the problems late at night after work. It is impossible to do them in the day when my abilities are keener (trust me). The weekends are better, however. I can see why you make a pass over the same problems seven times. It's starting to make sense.'

In this email Cuzear exhibited one of the key components of success, in this or any other field: the ability to select a successful path and then stick to it, no matter how difficult it becomes. If you have never studied tactical puzzles, then you may be frustrated, as Cuzear was. However, like Cuzear, if you want to be successful then you should stick with the program until you have seen it through.

Cuzear also notes that many players say that they want to improve but then they do nothing to improve. I am always amazed to see on the Internet chess server players who have played over 10, 000 games and still have very low ratings. If instead of playing so many games these players focused on improving their play, they would play less error prone chess and, presumably, enjoy playing chess even more.

Most recently, Cuzear sent me the following enthusiastic email:

'I thought I would give you a holler, I'm now a B player! I'm almost done with the Seven Circles. Wasn't able to do it in the time frame you recommended, but I've stuck with it and I'm hurting people with tactical vision. I'm on the 5th circle. I've had my share of debates with Master players who think they know what's important. There is a lot of other good stuff to tell you about. How your article has motivated a few people and we have study sessions every Friday night exploring the world of tactics. My students are beating the students of Master teachers. Just recently two of my students got top honours, one of them scoring 5/5 in the latest tourney and beating the number one state player in his age group. All I do is emphasise tactics. Also, I hold them to it. Two weeks ago my student, 9 years old Louis, played in a ten-minute tourney at the club. He came close to beating a strong speed player (1900+) when he failed to see the mate and lost on time. But throughout the game he used tactical vision and clearly outplayed his opponent. The dad wanted me to teach openings and I refused. Now the dad is in seventh heaven. He said he hardly recognised his son's and daughter's game since they developed a dynamic style.'

As you can see, Cuzear achieved a significant ratings gain (over 100 points!) before he was even finished with the Seven Circles program. You too will experience such improvements if you have the willpower to stick with the program.

Some chess commentators have suggested that after having played serious tournament chess for eight years, a player will have reached his peak and improvement will be almost impossible. This thesis is most commonly attributed to GM Andy Soltis, who wrote an article in *Chess Life* entitled 'You're Never Too Old To Mate' in which he claimed that very few players improved more than 100 points after playing seriously for eight years. Cuzear's example gives the lie to this chess 'law'. Cuzear spent over eight years stuck in Class C/Class D and shot up to Class B almost immediately after having implemented the Rapid Chess Improvement program. Anyone can do it!

# David's Story: Best Game of my Life

David is typical of many players who have found success with the Rapid Chess Improvement program. He is a young professional who had been stuck in a rut following traditional chess study practices, but his abilities soared once he started following the Rapid Chess Improvement path. David started off rated 1400 to 1500 and saw clear improvement in his abilities.

Shortly after I began describing my Rapid Chess Improvement theories, David sent me the following email:

'I was fascinated by your ... study program for the adult class player. I would seem to be the perfect guinea pig for your suggested program: I'm a 35 year-old trial attorney from Chicago who began studying and playing chess about 5 years ago. My present rating is around 1475 USCF (it was 1519, but I just had a bad tournament, as usual).

If you'll forgive a bit of personal history: On my daily train ride I typically study chess at least 30 minutes each day. I play a g/30 on the internet twice a week on my lunch hour and a ladder tournament game (g/90) at the local club once per week. I have played through every move of Silman's *Reassess Your Chess* and *Amateur's Mind* twice through, and have a reasonably strong understanding of typical endgames. I probably own seventy chess books, and have read a fair portion of most of them. I even spent two years trying to come up with an integrated opening repertoire (and finally gave up in disgust). Despite this, my strength has languished at its present level for at least two years, making study seem pointless. However, I love chess and figure that if I learned to try complex commodities fraud cases and capital homicides, I should be able to make 1700-1800 USCF with five years of study. Obviously, I'm studying the wrong things. (Sorry for the essay: I'm just venting).

I intend to try your program, since your essay makes excellent sense, and I'd settle for arriving at the lofty perch of 1600! Again, thanks for the interesting article. It gave me hope!'

David is very typical of many adult class players. He is a smart, highly trained professional who obviously has demonstrated the determination, intelligence, and diligence to stick with long term study plans. However, he was frustrated by his chess studies and saw no improvement. This was not David's fault – he simply did not have a study plan that was effective. Reading through Silman's Reassess Your Chess multiple times will not be helpful if you are dropping pieces. Silman is useful once you have learned how to calculate the short tactical sequences that you will learn through chess vision and Seven Circles.

After working on the chess vision drills for just one day David sent me the following email:

'By the way, nothing like quick success to breed enthusiasm for a new program. My local club is currently playing a USCF-rated club championship, and I played last night. If anyone questions the effectiveness or worth of your 'micro drills' concept, send them to me. I did my first set of micro drills yesterday afternoon, then played an expert last night. I saw two tactical sequences based on forks and skewers I had just learned in the micro drills. In a complex (for me) tactical battle, I won an exchange based entirely on my newly-discovered 'Chess Vision', and was disappointed to only draw the game in a time scramble. It was probably the best game of my life. I hope this is the start of a trend.'

David's success with the chess vision drills is exceptional. In just one day he was able to improve his abilities enough to draw against an expert rated over 500 points higher. Although this is unusual, if you have never experienced the power of doing chess vision drills you will be delighted by how much your skills improve.

Once he had spent a little bit more time with the system David had a rich set of successful experiences:

'I thought you would find my last month's adventures with your system interesting. I have finished the first month's suggestions, and have started a mini seven cycles. I can only study during the week, so I'm doing the first 400 problems in CT-ART 3.0 at an accelerated rate (an excellent suggestion). I'll then do two additional cycles with the harder problems.

A summary of my recent games (all game/100 and rated):

Game 1 – I won against a 1200 with a simple combo on move 5 that won a piece (love that 'chess vision'!);

Game 2 – I drew with a 2050 after he made two tactical errors that I actually saw (again: love that 'chess vision,' although I couldn't convert a R+P v B+2P endgame in time pressure);

Game 3 – I lost to a 1900 when I dropped a pawn in the opening and lost a piece trying to wriggle out of the disaster I'd created;

Game 4 – I drew a quiet game with a 2209 in which I avoided several tactical mistakes but missed a piece that he hung to a three move combo (Fritz 6 sure knows how to deflate you!);

Game 5 – I barely beat a 1400 who outplayed me completely until he made a tactical mistake in a R+P endgame ('chess vision' to the rescue);

Game 6 – I drew a wild game with a 2100 in which I survived a nasty kingside attack, then won a pawn based on a simple pin he overlooked, then made a tactical mistake in time pressure, which should have dropped a rook, then converted the mistake into a Q for 2 rooks, then agreed to a time pressure draw when I had a three move win of a rook. Ouch!

Since this is completely atypical of my play and I probably gained 50 points, I must give your system all the credit. Wow. I might actually make 1800 someday :-)'

David's estimated improvement can be seen by calculating his tournament performance rating:

| Opponent's rating | Win/Loss | Performance |
|:---:|:---:|:---:|
| 1200 | W | 1600 |
| 2050 | D | 2050 |
| 1900 | L | 1500 |
| 2209 | D | 2209 |
| 1400 | W | 1800 |
| 2100 | D | 2100 |

The average performance rating is 1876.5, a stunning achievement for a player rated 1400-1500. At the World Open, I won the U2000 section as a 1915 and my performance rating was approximately 2200, approximately 300 points greater than my actual rating. David outperformed his rating by over 350 points in his tournament.

In another email David wrote: 'I put together a rough program for endgames based on your system, and it has improved my endgame play tremendously, especially in time pressure.'

Unfortunately, because of work commitments David was not able to stay with the Rapid Chess Improvement program. However, he has now found a way to rapidly improve and if he does choose to return to the game, he will no longer have to waste time on methods that do not work.

# The story of Aaron Schlepler: Instant 100 points

Aaron first wrote to tell me that he had hit upon the idea of studying tactics in a structured way himself after focusing on other facets of his game:

'Like you, I began playing chess as an adult. I have just completed my first year of play and have gone from absolute beginner to a rating of about 1420 USCF. (I have to estimate based on my Chess.net rating, which supposedly utilises the USCF ratings formula. I haven't yet played any OTB chess.) During that first year, I did not have a very systematic study approach. I worked through two books: Seirawan's *Winning Chess Tactics* (twice, in fact) and *Winning Chess Strategies*. I picked up the rudiments of endgame play using *Pandolfini's Endgame Course*. Slowly but steadily I began to improve.

But I was still losing a lot of games and it was getting very frustrating. I started looking for new ways to get better. Not long ago, after analysing some games using Fritz, I realised that I just wasn't strong enough tactically. I was missing so many tactical opportunities – both mine and those of my opponents. So I bought this CD from ChessBase called 'George Renko's Intensive Tactics Course'. I now work about an hour a day on tactics. After only six weeks and about 1200 exercises under my belt, my play has already improved. Although your article proposes a slightly different approach, I think the idea is the same. You must study tactics – every day, religiously – in order to improve. What matters most, I think, is having a structured plan and sticking to it.'

George Renko's Intensive Tactics Course can be purchased from ChessBase (www.chessbase.com). The course is only a little less expensive than CT-ART and does not have its excellent training features. However, if you already have that program and do not want to spring for CT-ART, it is an adequate substitute which is certainly better than any book since Fritz can be used to analyse the positions.

Even after focusing on tactics himself, Aaron found that using the Seven Circles approach was particularly useful:

'You and I exchanged several e-mails a few months back regarding your article. I finally did the Seven Circles, using CT-ART 3.0. I did 500 problems rather than

1000 because it fits with my schedule a little better – I'd almost never have eight hours to spend doing chess problems. I used the first 500, which made the most difficult problem a level 30. At first, some of the level 30 problems were quite difficult for me, but by the end they seemed way too easy. So I've devised a second 500-problem set that uses harder problems and proportioned them in such a way that it's almost a mini version of the 1200-problem set. Now I'm working on a second Seven Circles run. In terms of overall growth, I think it will be more useful.

Anyway, my tactical play has improved considerably, even having done these easier problems. I'm finding now that when Fritz analyses my games, it's finding fewer and fewer mistakes and missed opportunities. Of course, playing accurately doesn't always guarantee a win, but it helps. My rating on Chess.net has shot up over 100 points so far. I expect even more improvement after I go through the next set of problems seven times.'

The first 500 problems in CT-ART are quite simple. The fact that Aaron saw significant improvement – 100 points – after working through them is a testament to the importance of drilling simple tactical problems at the class level. By doing 500 problems instead of 1000 you can cut the total time to work through Seven Circles in half. The disadvantage, of course, is that you are unlikely to experience the ratings increase that the full Seven Circles would produce.

I asked Aaron for more information about his success and he replied:

'I may have a game or two that I am proud of. I like the ones where Fritz annotates moves '!!' and '!'. It's really amazing, but since I've done the Seven Circles, I have at least one of those games a week, whereas in the past it was really a rarity. The strength of the Seven Circles is that it helps you find particular moves that are very strong that you wouldn't have seen otherwise – moves that help you win a piece, say, or that lead to pawn promotion or something along those lines. I don't feel like there are many true combinations in my games.

I'll give you a little more information about my progress. I have determined that my rating has improved about 220-250 points over the last calendar year. And most of that has come in the last eight months. It was on March 1st, 2001, that I started studying tactics religiously. After doing the Seven Circles, I saw an instant 100-point increase in my rating. So nearly half of my improvement over the last year has been due in part to the Seven Circles. I'm doing my second run through it right now, this time using harder problems. I just started Circle 2.'

At the beginning of this book we defined rapid chess improvement to be 200 points over a one-year period. Aaron achieved that improvement with the help of the Seven Circles program.

## The Story of Jericho Barimen: Amazing things are happening in my head

Jericho Barimen modified the Rapid Chess Improvement program to fit his lifestyle:

'I just wanted to say that your [Rapid Chess Improvement program] is GREAT!

When I was reading [about your program] I felt that all the problems concern me. It's just exactly the way you say: I blunder all of the time during the course of the chess game. I try to read different books, but most of them are too difficult or just focused on something I do not understand. I took individual classes with a few IMs, but they are too good and they think I know the basics and somehow I had the feeling during the lesson that the guy was thinking, 'What a moron! How can he be so ignorant? This stuff is obvious and basic.' Well, for me it was not!

And your article was the first thing that was 'normal'. I am 27. I played chess when I was a kid and in school, but it was rare and rather for fun. I started playing a month ago and ... I had no idea that chess is such a bitch to learn.

I am not ranked in chess. I just want to learn to play so I would not be ashamed of my play. I went to a local tournament, but I lost almost every game. I blundered here, blundered there and so that was it. I won only one game and that's only because my opponent gave up the game after he lost a piece. He should have continued; I would surely have blundered and given him a win!

Your 5-month program seems too long for me. I cut it into 2 weeks. I decided I would do it all at once... Do you think it is a good approach? I want to spend time daily and do the following:

1) Concentric Square exercise (repeat for 14 days)

2) Knight Sight exercise (repeat for 14 days)

3) Problems, I have CT-ART 2.0 which I think is fine.

I picked 400 problems and I do them on a 8-4-2-1 basis for 14 days. I will see how it goes; maybe I will make it longer if I find it hard to follow. Maybe I will do 8-6-4-2-1.'

Jericho's experience with chess coaches is common among adult class players. Titled players see things instantly that class players have difficulty seeing. Because they do not have to go through the same conscious thought processes that class players have to go through, they have difficulty explaining what they can see in one glance at the board. The Rapid Chess Improvement program can be executed entirely on your own, without the help of a chess coach.

I think that Jericho's approach is a bit too extreme. Doing concentric squares, knight sight, and the tactical problems simultaneously over a period of fourteen days seems far too short a period. There is a danger that if you follow such a shortened version of the program, you will not see significant improvement and will become discouraged. Remember, achieving improvement in chess or any other field will require effort. If you are searching for a quick fix, you will not find it here. Rapid Chess Improvement is fast compared to other study programs but it is not instant.

However, this approach did seem to work for Jericho. In a later email he wrote:

'First of all I want to let you know that your *great* [system] was the first 'sane' thing I have read about chess. It just hits the point so perfectly!!!

You can't believe how much it helps me. The 'chess sight' exercises are key for me. It lets me develop this vision you talk about...

As I told you, I set a plan for 14 days for me. I combine part 1 of your article with part 2. Yes, maybe it is a strain for me, but I want quick results and I will work hard for these 14 days (2 weeks). I am amazed by the results so far! I am able to spot simple things on the chessboard during my games. Things, which I would *never expect myself to spot!!!* This is *only* thanks to your great article!!!

I spend 2 hours daily on your exercises.

1) I do the 'Concentric Square' exercise (but only with the rook, no other pieces involved yet).

2) Next I do the 'Knight Sight' exercise, but only squares which the knight attacks, no knight moves yet. I want to make myself comfortable with the basics first, before I move on.

3) I do 50 chess problems. These are simple solutions from CT-ART 2.0, the program I have.

Yesterday (for example) it took me 1 hour and 15 minutes to do 50 problems, averaging at 1.5 minutes per problem. It is a severe strain, but I want to push forward. I have 400 chess problems and I want to do them on a 8-4-2-1 basis. I will see how it goes; maybe I will make it last longer if I cannot cope with this speed. So far it's going okay. Amazing things are happening with my head. This is similar to if you are a small boy, who grows very rapidly and you measure your height every month and you see you are a few centimetres higher month after month!!!'

Jericho's dedication to the program – working two hours a day – is part of his success. You should be willing to set aside that much time to follow through the Rapid Chess Improvement exercises as well.

When Jericho had worked on the chess vision drills for just a short period of time he wrote:

'After the simple drills I noticed that I started to look at the chessboard a little bit differently. I mean before I just looked at the board and saw pawns and pieces, just like that. Right now I slowly start to see all the relations. It's like everything is on the board, thousand of lines and relations, and I kinda do not focus on one piece or pawn, but rather all at once.'

This is a good deooription of the chess vision that you will develop as you go through the very simple chess vision drills. Personally, I began to dream about positions at night and during the day random chess positions would pop into my head. This is evidence that your brain is working hard to assimilate the new capabilities that the Rapid Chess Improvement develops.

Make sure that you do not skimp on these chess vision drills – they will make it much easier to work through the Seven Circles and will pay great dividends when you experience time crunches during your games.

## Other Comments

In addition to the detailed case histories you have just read, dozens of other chess players have written to tell me about the benefits of working through the Rapid Chess Improvement program. Here are some of their comments.

'I would like to thank you for creating your systematic chess... I am totally stunned and surprised about this whole new idea – and I will of course try it myself!'

*Torsten Hellmann*

'Alexander Pope once wrote :

True wit is nature to advantage dress'd

What oft was thot, but ne'er so well express'd.

This applies perfectly to your outstanding '400 Points' piece. It's the best writing on chess that I've seen in a long time.

Aside from the practical value, it also took me back on a nostalgia trip. In 1976 I wrote *How to Win at Racquetball* from the point of view of the mediocre athlete. A short time later *Sports Illustrated* asked me to do their book on racquetball strategy in spite of the fact that I was not a celebrity in the sport. They said: The pros simply do not understand the problems of the club player.'

*Victor Spear*
author of *Sports Illustrated Racquetball* and *How to Win at Racquetball*

'[The Rapid Chess Improvement program] really hit home for me because I've been reading a lot of chess books lately and feel I have a lot of chess knowledge (for someone who started playing seriously three months ago), but not much chess ability. As an example, one of my opponents commented that I had a strong positional sense. He said this right after he had beaten me in a game where I had slowly been building up an advantage, but had lost the game due to two or three tactically poor moves.

I also have a terrible time with time. It is so bad that none of my friends will play against me without a clock. It takes me a long time to consider moves. I think this is because I'm slow at calculating tactical situations and I'm familiar with a lot of positional information that I've never put into practice, so it takes me a long time to go through all the half-learnt positional aspects of a position.

My chess experience reminds me a lot of how I learned basic arithmetic. When I was taught addition my teacher wanted us to practice with flash-cards and to do practice problems. One day, while doing some of the practice problems, my grandmother showed me that you could add by counting dots on imaginary dominoes. This method will give the correct answer, but is much slower than the kind of instant recall I would have had if I had stuck with the flash-cards. Throughout my education I always hated the rote learning exercises and spent all my effort on understanding new concepts. Looking back now I can see how skipping the rote exercises made learning the concepts harder.

Anyway, to make a long story short, I'm sold. I don't care anymore whether a king, bishop and pawn vs. king, knight and rook is a won or drawn game. I'm going to learn one white opening, a couple of moves into the popular defences to that opening and one king pawn and one queen pawn black defence and no more positional generalities until I've got my tactics down cold.

I tried your Concentric Square exercise before going to the local chess club last week. Mostly my results were typical for me; either losing on time from a winning position or playing blunder-per-move push-the-wood-at-random chess. However, against one guy I beat him three times in a row, all with a series of tactical moves. Things were just falling into place. I was making quick moves that didn't have big holes in them (or none that my opponent saw). The last two games of the night I played against my strongest regular opponent and beat him twice at 5-minute chess. Again I was just 'seeing things' and was able to play at a much faster rate than normal.

When I went through the Concentric Square exercise I noticed that I missed some forks. That is, I would notice, say, a fork along two diagonals and not be able to remember seeing one on a previous symmetrical position. I thought it would be helpful to go through the exercise and count how many forks and skewers are possible in each position and write them down so that I could double check that I didn't miss any squares as I go through each time. Instead of trying to count on a real chessboard and not having a way to go back (if I thought I'd missed a square on an earlier set-up), I did the whole exercise by creating board positions in ChessBase Light. That way I can go back easily and see if I missed anything. The way I do it is to place a queen on all the squares where she can fork or skewer, and place a white king somewhere off the black rook's file and rank to make ChessBase happy. I plan to print all the positions out and use them as flash-cards (as well as do the exercise in the way you suggested). I'm also thinking of finding a tool (maybe ChessBase Light will do this) that will let me place arrows on diagrams and create a bunch of flash-cards showing the moves of the pieces from various positions. I could also modify the fork/skewer positions to show crossing arrows instead of the queens.'

*Rich Van Gaasbeck*

Note that the program that Rich mentions, ChessBase Light, is available as a free download form www.chessbase.com.

The very rapid improvement that Rich saw in his playing capabilities – after just one session – is not unheard of, but it is unusual. Different players will react to these drills differently, but every class player will benefit from going through them. They are the foundation upon which tactical vision is built. So do not be concerned if you do not see the immediate change in your abilities that Rich experienced. Rest assured that you are improving and continue with the five-month program.

'I've been kicking around chess for almost 25 years. I have tons of books. I have tons of computers. I have taken lessons from Masters. I have to tell you that your [Rapid Chess Improvement program] is without a doubt the most insightful, brilliant, refreshing and original approach to chess training I have ever encountered!'

*David Ridge*

I cannot convey in words how much satisfaction I experienced this morning after reading part one of your plan. I am a 48-year-old who did not play any chess until a few years ago. I have had a Class D rating all that time, and now hopefully will see some real improvement in my chess playing ability.

*James Babkes*

Thanks for the wonderful [program]. I coach a highly successful high school team, but have struggled with inexperienced players whose lack of board and tactical vision impedes any attempt to teach higher level concepts and skills. They ultimately develop this vision, but it seems to take forever. Thanks for the drills... I will begin using them this afternoon and look forward to your continuing contributions to the CC.

*Neil Gleason (1941 USCF)*

I think you may have a significant impact on a number of people with your article. I think it will become a great contribution to the chess world.

*Mark Kaprielian (1577 USCF)*
*President, MetroWest Chess Club*
*Vice President, Massachusetts Chess Association*

I found your [program] fascinating. It's original and thought provoking, and very well written.

*James Krycka (1114 USCF)*

I have just finished reading [your Rapid Chess Improvement program]: it is wonderful!

*Gary Kolks*
*Chemistry PhD*

Excellent!

*NM Spencer Lower (2295 USCF)*

I very much enjoyed reading your [Rapid Chess Improvement program]...this was a very well written article.

*Alan Hodge (981 USCF)*
*Professional copy editor*

I read your [Rapid Chess Improvement program] and really enjoyed it. I think that it will be a great help to me.

*Brian Summer*

Thank you for your work thus far. I am an older adult who took up chess in my 50s and am still rated less than my first provisional rating of 1450 some 10 years ago. Yet I can now name perhaps ten openings and follow them for over ten moves. Something's wrong.

*Edward Beardshear (1395 USCF)*

## Summary

In this chapter you have read about the experiences of a dozen players who have experienced the Rapid Chess Improvement program. Their success illustrates what you can achieve by following the program.

A few things stand out from these stories. First, all of the players who stuck with the plan experienced significant improvement. Second, the advantages of using CT-ART (which you can order from www.chessassistant.com) were mentioned by several of the players. If at all possible, you should choose this program – or another one like it – for the Seven Circles exercises. Cuzear Ford went so far as to say that he could not imagine working through the study program without the use of CT-ART.

Third, working on the chess vision drills provides immediate benefits. Jericho Barimen saw changes in his thought processes after just a few days of doing the chess vision drills.

These inspirational stories suggest that the method described in this book can work for many adult class players. If you follow the program, you too will experience the excitement experienced by these players. If you find that your enthusiasm starts to wane, revisit this section and read about the victories achieved by your fellow class players.

# Chapter Six

# Moving On...

If you have successfully followed the five-month program described in this book, you are well on your way to becoming an Expert. I became an Expert approximately a year after completing the Rapid Chess Improvement program without making any marked changes to the way I studied. During that period of time my rating went up on a regular basis with no significant setbacks.

In this chapter I share with you some thoughts on becoming an Expert and some preliminary ideas on what I would do to become a Master.

## Current Theories

At the beginning of this book, I discussed the various chess improvement methods that are aimed at class players. Before outlining what I believe is necessary to become an Expert or a Master, let us examine what the prevailing wisdom is on how to become a titled player.

IM Ignacio Marin has an excellent web page which can be found at http://cmgm.stanford.edu/~marin/SCA9.html. There he identifies three key ingredients to becoming a Master:

> 1) Play as frequently as possible and against strong players.
>
> 2) Analyse your games.
>
> 3) Study tactics.

I broadly agree with these three ideas. Elsewhere in this book, I have already shared how I believe that class players should analyse their games. To summarise, the games should be analysed using a computer program, such as Fritz. You should focus on the areas of the evaluation graph that show the largest changes against you and try to understand how to modify your thinking to prevent these large changes from occurring in the future.

Marin's third idea – studying tactics – is, of course, the primary subject of this book. I am happy to see that Marin believes that this is an effective method of chess improvement even beyond the class level.

The only suggestion that I would modify in any serious way is the first one. When I began playing chess, I played exclusively in open tournaments and would often finish with scores of ½/4 and 1/5. I found this very demoralising and had difficulty putting my best effort into each game.

Instead, I suggest trying to play against opponents who are no more than 200 points stronger than you are, so I would modify Marin's statement to read: 'Try to play against opponents who are stronger than you are, but not by more than 200 points.'

You can do this most easily by entering class tournaments and playing either at your level, if you happen to be at the low end of a class, or by playing at the next higher level if you happen to be near the top of the class.

In an article on KasparovChess.com, IM Valery Tsaturian wrote that to become a chess professional 'you should arm yourself with patience, as the way from an amateur to the professional of an international level (ELO of 2400, or even Grandmaster) will take you 4-5 years.' I find this estimate of how long it takes to become a strong player ridiculously low. Below I estimate that it would take me a total of six years to become a Master (ELO=2100). My guess is that it would take me close to ten years to improve from an ELO of 2100 to an ELO of 2400, assuming that no mental deterioration takes place during that time. Since such deterioration would almost certainly take place, I doubt that I would be able to achieve an ELO of 2400 no matter how hard I tried.

Tsaturian goes on to say that you should 'prepare the opening repertoire of a professional player', learn 'typical strategic and tactical moves', 'learn standard methods of playing the most frequent endings', and 'play 300-350 games against strong chess players and analyse them in detail.'

Tsaturian is aiming his advice at a level much higher than Master – he is giving advice to someone who wants to become a chess professional. Certainly a Master does not need to spend an inordinate amount of time on opening study or on endgames. I do agree that playing and analysing several hundred games and learning tactical sequences is of great importance.

In *How to be a Class A Player*, Alex Dunne writes: 'If you wish to improve your chess, you do not go out and challenge the World Champion to a match. Rather, you would find a player who is only a little better than you to play and you would play him until you learned from him and beat him. That is the way to improve.' I agree that this is an excellent way to test your skills. If you play an opponent who is too strong, then he will outplay you in every aspect of the game and focusing on areas to improve will be difficult.

However, if you play against an opponent who is only slightly better than you are then the game will be exciting, challenging, and educational.

## Becoming an Expert

I did not make any significant modifications to the chess vision drills and the Seven Circles exercise when I made the transition from Class A player to Expert. For me, this transition took ten months and involved learning a little bit about the opening (using the technique described below) and changing my chess style to suit my tactical ability.

## The One Move a Game Opening Study Program

I do not suggest studying openings until you are a Class A player, but if you absolutely must I suggest the one move a game opening study program. In this program you simply analyse your games with Fritz or another computer program and, if you make a significant mistake very early in the game, then you look up the opening you played, find when you deviated from the standard line, and then change your opening to reflect what you have discovered.

For example, consider the diagram below, which arose after 1 e4 e5 2 ♘f3 ♘c6 3 ♗b5 f5 4 ♘c3 fxe4 5 ♘xe4 (see following diagram). Here I played 5...♘ge7?, which is not a book move. After 6 ♘fg5 ♘d4?? 7 ♕h5+ wins the game on the spot. Here a mistake in the opening combined with a serious tactical error led to an immediate loss.

By using Fritz's auto-annotation feature, I can see that the preferred fifth moves for Black in this line are 5...♘f6 and 5...d5. I prefer 5...d5 so I added this single move to my opening repertoire. I did not study this line further nor did I study alternate moves for Black prior to the fifth move. I simply noted where I had deviated from Master play and changed just one move so that next time I would avoid the mistake that I had made in this game.

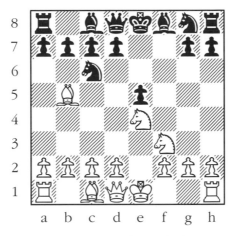

*Chamberlain-de la Maza. Black to move.*
*Here I played 5...♘ge7?, a move that is not played in master level games.*

Why does this method of studying the openings work? First, because each game leads to at most one small change in your opening repertoire, you do not need to spend hours studying opening lines or ideas. Memorising opening lines is very de-motivating and does little to help your overall chess ability. Second, since you have just made a mistake early in the game you will be interested in learning how a Master would play in that same position. You will find it easy to learn and memorise your new move. Third, by changing your repertoire slowly you will be able to adjust to the new moves you learn and fit your repertoire to your style.

Will you learn a lot about the opening using this method? No, you will not. But you will learn more than enough to become an Expert. For example, when I became an Expert the longest opening line I knew was just eight moves and for most of the openings I played I just knew a handful moves. In total, my entire opening repertoire consisted of fewer than 100 positions!

Although this method is very simple and straightforward – it takes less than fifteen minutes per game – I do not recommend it until you are a Class A player (USCF 1800+) and are working on becoming an Expert. Until you reach the 1800 level you should continue to work on your tactical ability by focusing on chess vision drills and Seven Circles.

## Continue to Study Tactics

In my experience, strong Class A players and weak Experts (a range that encompasses ratings between 1950 and 2050) still make significant tactical errors during their games.

As such, you will be able to take advantage of the chess vision drills and Seven Circles to continue to improve your play. Here is an example of the tactical opportunities that abound:

□ **De la Maza (1834)**
■ **Armes (2108)**

**1 e4 e5 2 ♘f3 ♘c6 3 d4 exd4 4 c3 ♘f6 5 e5 ♘e4 6 ♗d3 d5 7 0-0 ♗g4 8 cxd4 ♗e7 9 ♘c3 ♗xf3 10 ♕xf3 ♘g5 11 ♗xg5 ♗xg5 12 ♖fd1 ♘xd4 13 ♗b5+ ♘xb5 14 ♘xb5 0-0 15 ♖xd5 ♕e7 16 ♖ad1 ♖fd8 17 ♖xd8+ ♖xd8 18 ♖xd8+ ♕xd8 19 h4 ♗c1 20 ♕xb7 ♗xb2 21 ♕e4 (see Diagram) 21...a6 22 ♘xc7 f6 23 e6 ♗e5 24 ♘d5 ♕d6 25 e7 ♔f7 26 ♕c4 g6 27 ♕c8 Black resigns**

In this game Armes, an Expert player, makes several tactical errors which lose the game, the most surprising of which is 21...a6??, which simply drops a pawn to a two-move combination (see the diagram below). The queen cannot retake after 22 ♘xc7 because there is a back rank mate.

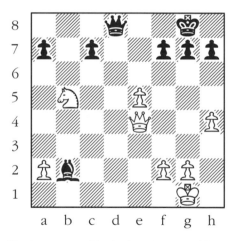

*de la Maza-Armes. Black to move. Black played 21...a6?? which immediately drops a pawn to a two move back rank combination. Armes is an Expert and this error shows that even at this level tactical study is critical.*

The evaluation graph (see Figure 34) shows that Armes continued to weaken his position by at least half a point per move for the next several moves. His very next move 22...f6, for example, gives White a passed pawn.

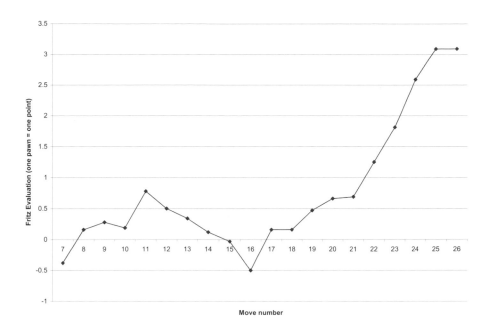

Move number

*Figure 34: de la Maza-Armes. Armes, an Expert,*
*makes a serious tactical error with 21...a6??*

If you are able to rub out this sort of error from your game, you will be that much closer to playing at Expert level.

So to make the transition from Class A player to Expert, find the hardest tactical problems that you can and construct a Seven Circles drill using them. Also, continue to find tactical errors in your own games and create chess vision drills to help you overcome these blind spots in your game.

## Becoming a Master

One of the truisms of chess, as well as any other field, is that as you get closer and closer to the top, improvement becomes harder and harder. If you run the 100-yard dash in twenty seconds, reducing your time to nineteen seconds is not that difficult. But if you run the 100-yard dash in ten seconds improving your time to 9 seconds or even to 9.5 seconds is extremely difficult.

In chess, I roughly estimate that the amount of time required to improve your rating from 2000 (the cut-off for Expert) to 2200 (the cut-off for Master) is double the amount of time that it takes you to reach the 2000 level.

When I started playing chess I was rated approximately 1300 and when I finished playing two years later I was rated approximately 2000. So, according to my rule, this means that it would take approximately four years of working 2-3 hours per day to improve to the Master level. This is no small commitment of time or effort.

However, note that since I am not a Master myself the suggestions that I give here are completely speculative. But they are based on a close examination of how Master level players play the game.

We can begin to understand Master level play by looking at a game between two strong Experts.

□ **Desmarais (2187)**
■ **Warfield (2160)**

**1 d4 d5 2 c4 e6 3 ♘c3 ♗e7 4 ♘f3 ♘f6 5 ♗g5 0-0 6 e3 h6 7 ♗h4 b6 8 ♗xf6 ♗xf6 9 cxd5 exd5 10 b4 c6N 11 ♗e2 a5 12 b5 c5 13 ♖c1 ♗e6 14 dxc5 bxc5 15 ♘a4 c4 16 ♘c3 a4 17 ♘d4 ♕a5 18 0-0 a3 19 f4 g6 20 f5 gxf5 21 ♘xe6 fxe6 22 ♘xd5 exd5 23 ♕xd5+ ♔h8 24 ♗xc4 ♖a7 25 ♖xf5 ♕b6 26 ♖cf1 ♕xe3+ 27 ♔h1 ♘d7 28 h3 ♕e7 29 ♗b3 ♖aa8 30 ♕d2 ♗g7 31 ♖f7 ♕e8 32 ♖e1 ♘e5 33 ♖xf8+ ♕xf8 34 ♕d5 ♖d8 35 ♕e4 ♘d3 36 ♖e2**

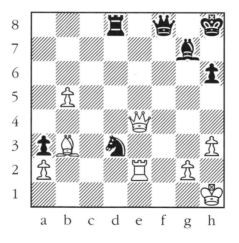

**36...♘f2+**

Although this wins material, it is a blunder which allows White to snatch a draw. After 36...♘c5 Black would be winning easily.

**37 ♖xf2 ♕xf2 38 ♗c2 ♔g8 39 ♗b3+ ♔h8 40 ♗c2 ♔g8 41 ♗b3+ ½-½**

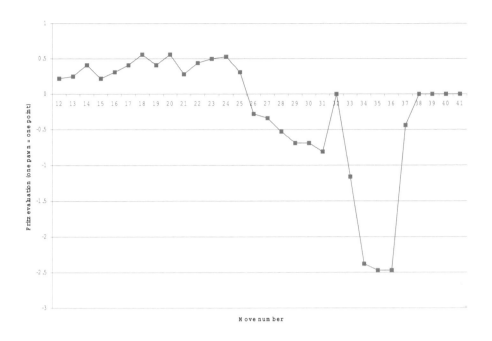

*Figure 35: Desmarais-Warfield.*
*The graph shows sharp changes, indicating that both players made significant tactical errors even though they are both strong Experts.*

Desmarais is now a Master while Warfield is an experienced Expert. A chart of Fritz's evaluation graph for this game is shown in Figure 35.

The graph shows sharp changes, proving that even strong Experts can make significant tactical errors. This suggests that even at the strong Expert level, tactical study is critical.

If we examine a game between two Masters rated approximately 100 points above these two strong Experts, we also see evidence of significant tactical errors.

☐ **Godin (2200)**
■ **Cherniak (2254)**

**1 c4 e5 2 g3 ♘c6 3 ♗g2 g6 4 ♘c3 ♗g7 5 e4 d6 6 ♘ge2 h5 7 d3 h4 8 f3 f5 9 ♗e3 ♗h6 10 ♗f2 ♘f6 11 ♘d5 0-0 12 ♘xf6+ ♕xf6 13 gxh4 fxe4 14 dxe4 ♗g4 15 0-0 ♗xf3 16 ♗xf3 ♕xf3 17 ♘g3 ♗e3 18 ♕xf3 ♖xf3 19 ♗xe3 ♖xe3 20 ♖f6 ♖f8 21 ♖xg6+ ♔h7 22 h5 ♘d4 23 ♖f1 ♖f4 24 ♔g2 ♖d3 25 ♖xf4 exf4 26 ♘f5 ♖d2+ 27 ♔h3 f3 28 ♖g7+ ♔h8 29 ♖xc7 ♘e6 30 ♖c8+ ♔h7 31 ♔g3**

113

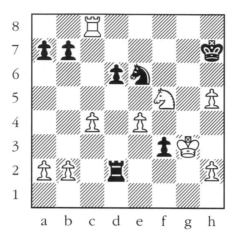

**31...♖xb2**

Black could have maintained the f-pawn with 31...f2. Now his position goes rapidly downhill.

**32 ♔xf3 ♖xa2 33 h4 a5 34 ♖e8 ♘c5 35 ♖e7+ ♔h8 36 ♘xd6 ♖b2 37 ♔g4 a4 38 ♔g5 a3 39 ♔h6 ♖g2 40 ♖e8+ Black resigns**

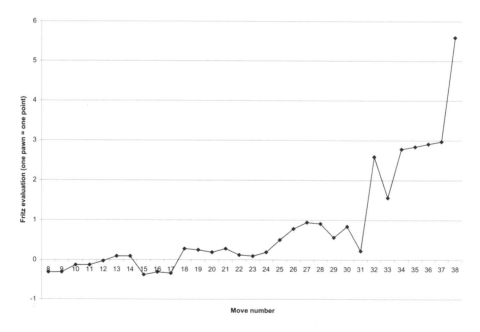

*Figure 36: Godin-Cherniak. Masters make significant tactical mistakes in their games, as illustrated by this evaluation graph.*

Compare these two graphs with Figure 37, a game between two top Grandmasters. There are far fewer big jumps in this game, suggesting that tactical ability continues to be critical as you progress from the Expert level to Master.

So, clearly, the first step in becoming a Master is to continue your tactical study. Find the hardest tactical problems that you can and use the Seven Circles method to work through them. *Test Your Chess IQ: Grandmaster Challenge* by August Livshitz and *John Nunn's Chess Puzzle Book* by John Nunn may come in handy at this stage. Also, you can now consider studying more specialised tactical books such as *Tactical Chess Endings* by John Nunn.

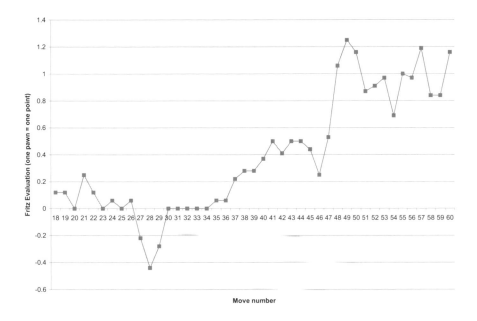

*Figure 37: Miles-Kramnik. Note how few squiggles there are.*
*There are no significant tactical errors in this game.*

## Playing Dangerously

In addition to continuing to study tactics, I believe that a critical part of becoming a Master is to develop a chess style. By chess style I mean a preferred style of playing. Do you prefer open positions to closed positions? Middlegames to endgames? Strategy to tactics?

Once you have developed a chess style you can focus all of your attention on (1) forcing the game into positions which suit your style and (2) further developing your abilities in that style.

If you have followed the chess vision drills and Seven Circles drill in this book and have made them the basis of your chess style you will prefer:

- open positions to closed positions
- unorthodox positions to well studied ones
- complicated middlegames
- simple openings to theoretical openings
- piece endgames to pawn endgames

This style of play has immediate implications for various aspects of your play. For example, you will almost certainly want to open 1 e4 and when following the One Move a Game Opening study method described above, you will want to steer the game into positions in which there are as few 25-move variations as possible.

This style of play has been practised by very strong GMs such as Shirov and Mikhail Tal. Writing about Shirov at KasparovChess.com, Eugene Atarov wrote:

'I think that, in any position, he looks for an opportunity to complicate the issue, make his opponent feel nervous, fidget on his (or her) chair and ... commit a mistake! Shirov's favourite trick is to transpose into unbalanced positions, where the usual chess rules and guidelines are not applicable.'

The great Rudolf Spielman wrote: 'A good sacrifice is one that is not necessarily sound but leaves your opponent dazed and confused.' World Champion Mikhail Tal voiced a similar opinion: 'You must take your opponent into a deep dark forest where 2+2=5, and the path leading out is only wide enough for one.'

Shirov plays and Spielman, Tal and others played a game that is qualitatively similar to the one that you will be able to play once you have worked through the chess vision drills and Seven Circles. Instead of relying on your understanding of middlegame strategy, openings and endgames to win games, you will be able to out-calculate your opponent. Hence, you will benefit from randomising the chess position where, as Atarov says, 'the usual chess rules and guidelines are not applicable.' This will nullify your opponent's knowledge and highlight your strengths.

Although Shirov is and Spielmann and Tal were, of course, great players who had a very deep understanding of chess, the attacking style can also be used by much weaker players to great advantage. At the 2001 World Open I had the opportunity to practice this philosophy in the seventh game. I was on the top board and with a win I had the opportunity to be in clear first place.

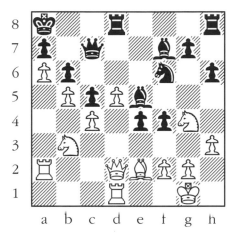

*Rosen-de la Maza, World Open 2001. Black now opens up the white kingside.*

In the position shown in the diagram, I had to decide how to launch an attack against White's kingside. Fritz's choices in this position, in order from best to worst are:

-0.72: ♖he8; -0.69: ♗g6; -0.66: h5; -0.63: ♕d6; -0.63: ♔b8; -0.59: ♖hg8; -0.59: ♖hf8, -0.50. ♗d6; -0.56: ♕e7; 0.47: ♘xg4; -0.41: ♕b8; -0.28: ♔g8; -0.09: f3

Remember that one pawn equals one point, so Fritz believes that the first move will give Black an advantage of approximately three-quarters of a point. I played 30...f3, a move which Fritz says is ranked thirteenth! Although a computer may consider this to be a blunder, it plays to Black's strengths. By opening up the f-file and the h2-b8 diagonal, Black will now be able to directly attack the king. White will be forced to defend move after move after move as Black swoops in along the file and the diagonal that this pawn sacrifice opens up. Note also that White's protected passed d-pawn gives him good opportunities in an endgame. Because this was a game I had to win to finish in clear first, the 30...f3 gamble was more than justified.

What happened in this game? After 30...f3 31 gxf3 ♘xg4 32 hxg4 ♗g6 33 fxe4 ♖hf8 34 ♕d3 ♕e7 35 ♗f3 ♕h4 36 ♖ad2 ♕h3 37 ♗g2 ♕xg4 38 ♘a1 ♗h5 39 ♖b1 ♕f4 40 ♘c2 ♖d6 (see next Diagram) White blundered with 41 ♕e3?? and quickly lost the game after 41...♕h2+ 42 ♔g1 ♗f4. See Figure 38 for the evaluation graph during these critical moves.

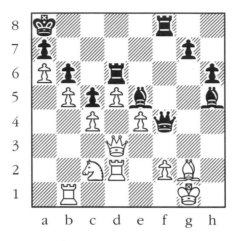

*Rosen-de la Maza, World Open 2001. White is about to blunder with 41 ♕e3??*

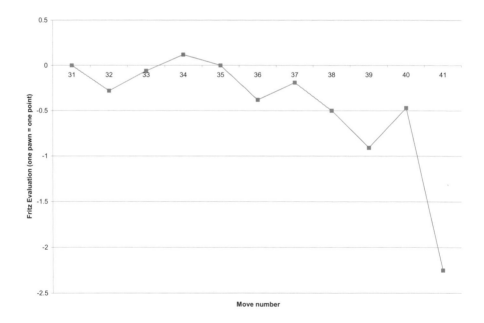

*Figure 38: Evaluation graph of Rosen-de la Maza from move 31 to move 41. After Black decided to sacrifice a pawn with 30...f3, Fritz evaluates the game to be even. But the pressure that this pawn sacrifice enabled caused White to make a game-losing mistake on move 41.*

This is a good example, at the class level, of taking an opponent down 'a deep dark forest' where only one will emerge the victor. The pressure for White was simply too great in this position. Move after move after move he had to find the right defence and he finally cracked.

Is Fritz's plan of attacking down the e-file with 30...♖he8 worse? No, Black is winning in that case as well. However, the attack down the e-file is, from the perspective of the class player, much less clear. It takes more time to develop and it allows ♘xe5. Removing black's bishop takes an important attacking piece off the board and developing the attack down the e-file poses a risk for Black because it takes some time to generate concrete threats.

In short, this is the sort of decision that a player must make during the game that gives him the opportunity to push the position on the board in a direction that favours his skills. Just as a baseball team will change pitchers depending on whether the batter is left handed or right handed, a chess player will be able to adjust his play depending on his relative advantage. This is what GM Igor Zaitsev means when he says. 'Thus, it turns out that in order to survive in modern chess it is much more important and necessary for a chess player to create (using all the means at his or her disposal and not caring very much about the perfection of his or her ideas) such a threshold of difficulty for a concrete opponent that the latter commits mistakes.' Although Zaitsev was aiming his comment at master level players, it applies equally well to class players who are working on becoming Masters.

## Piece Co-ordination

One of the most often heard chess maxims is: 'It is better to play with a bad plan than no plan at all.' In this book I have made the case that even if you do have a plan, if you are dropping pieces to short combinations, it will do you no good. So I would rewrite this slogan to read: 'It is better to see all three-move combinations than to have a good plan.'

This slogan will work until you are at least at the Expert level. I know this because I have succeeded in using very simple plans, like those discussed in the How to Think chapter, to beat Experts and have achieved an Expert rating myself.

But once you get to the strong Expert level and want to make the move to the Master level, you will find that your opponents make fewer and fewer tactical errors. You will have to start relying on piece co-ordination to create positions in which your tactical ability shines. For example, in Figure 38 we saw how a pawn sacrifice made it possible to immediately implement the plan of attacking the opponent's king.

Why are plans important? Certainly they are not necessary to play great chess. After all, chess programs do not plan, at least not in the traditional sense of the term that we use to describe human planning in chess, and they play at grandmaster level.

Plans are not intrinsically good, but they do force you to do something that is intrinsically good: co-ordinate your pieces. One of the greatest differences between class level play and master level play is that at the class level each piece often seems to exist in its own universe while at the master level all of the pieces on the board work together to achieve an objective.

Master level players are able to carry off splendid sacrificial attacks because all of their pieces are involved in the attack. In contrast, a class player may be able to calculate the same attack that the Master calculates – particularly if the class player has worked through the exercises in this book – but will often not be able to place his pieces in a position that allows the attack to take place in the first place.

I wish I knew how to develop piece co-ordination quickly and effectively. I do not, but one simple trick seems to help: choose a square to attack and then point all of your pieces in the direction of that square. Note that many positional concepts, such as the plan of doubling rooks on a file, are special cases of this particular idea.

Which are the best squares to control? Often the best squares are the centre squares and those around the king. When these two sets of squares are one and the same, the idea is particularly powerful. A reasonable example of this idea occurred in a game that I played in the fifth round of the 2001 World Open U2000 section. My opponent was up a pawn when I decided to use my advantage in development and my two bishops to control the centre squares.

My opponent underestimated the combinatorial possibilities and after losing a pawn quickly lost the game.

☐ **de la Maza (1915)**
■ **Madenci (1928)**

**1 e4 e6 2 c4 d5 3 d4 dxe4 4 ♘c3 ♗b4 5 ♘ge2 c5 6 a3 ♗xc3+ 7 ♘xc3 cxd4 8 ♘xe4 ♘f6 9 ♗d3 ♘xe4 10 ♗xe4 ♕a5+ 11 ♗d2 ♕e5 12 ♕e2 f5 13 ♗f3 ♕xe2+ 14 ♔xe2 ♔f7 (see Diagram)**

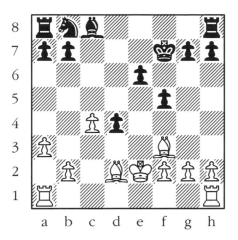

*de la Maza-Madenci. White to move. The position after 14...♔f7.*

15 ♗f4 ♔f6 16 ♗d6 ♖d8 17 c5 e5 18 ♗d5 ♘c6 19 ♖he1 ♘c7 20 ♗e1 ♗e6 21 ♗xe5+ ♔xe5 22 ♔f3+ ♔f6 23 ♖xe6+ ♔f7 24 ♖ae1 ♘g6 25 ♖b6+ ♔f8 26 ♖xb7 d3 27 ♖f7+ ♔g8 28 ♖xa7+ ♔f8 29 ♖f7+ ♔g8 30 ♖xf5+ ♔h8 31 ♖d5 d2 32 ♖d1 **Black resigns**

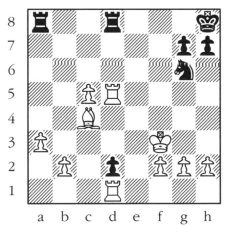

*de la Maza-Madenci. Final position...*

One critical position is shown in the diagram which occurs after 14...♔f7. White now stakes out a claim to the centre squares with his bishops while Black will try to control the centre with pawns.

All of white's moves are now designed to control the centre squares around

Black's king: 15 ♗f4 controls e5 and d6, 16 ♗d6 controls e7 and e5, 17 c5 controls d6 and protects the bishop, 18 ♗d5 controls e6, 19 ♖he1 controls the e file, 20 ♗c4 preserves the white bishop, and finally 21 ♗xe5+ leads to a white advantage. Note that three of white's four pieces – both bishops and the rook – were all organised with the simple goal of controlling the centre squares next to the black king. Later, White plays ♖ae1, bringing the final rook into the game with the goal of continuing to control the e-file.

This idea is powerful enough that even after White is clearly winning, the combination of the light-squared bishop on c4 with the rook on the sixth and seventh ranks proves devastating. The black king, which had been on e5, ends up on h8, losing a tempo on almost every move.

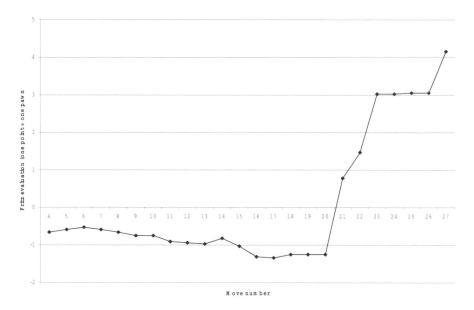

*Figure 39: de la Maza-Madenci. White is down a pawn early on but then implements a simple plan that will help co-ordinate his pieces: Control the central squares around the king. Thus White positions both of his bishops and one of his rooks to control the e-file. By move 21 this plan has paid dividends and a few moves later the game is over.*

Note that, according to Fritz's evaluation (Figure 39), White's position actually deteriorates for a few moves after move 14 while White positions his pieces to control critical squares on the e-file next to the king. In this sense this plan is similar to the one followed in Figure 38 in which a questionable pawn sacrifice first led to a decline in the evaluation before leading to a quick victory.

It is the ability to make these subtle trade-offs that distinguish the Master from the Expert. Making sure that your pieces are active and co-ordinated is an essential part of making the transition from class player to Master.

It is critical to remember that the plan itself is not what is important. What is important is to mobilise all of the pieces to achieve the same goal.

## Summary

In this section I've argued that, to a large degree, you can become an Expert and probably a Master by simply continuing the exercises that I've suggested earlier in this book. You should supplement this with some light opening study using the One Move a Game method.

You can also improve your ability to co-ordinate your pieces by choosing a small set of adjacent squares to attempt to control and then pointing all of your pieces towards those squares.

A final word of advice is to play games against players who are slightly stronger than you and then analyse them by using a chess program, focusing on those moves where the score moves against you the most.

# Solutions to Exercises

**Exercise 1:** 15...♖a8 16 ♕xb7 ♖b8, skewering the queen to the rook.

**Exercise 2:** 15 ♖xf8+ ♔xf8 16 ♕f2+ ♗f6 17 e5, picking off the d4-bishop.

**Exercise 3:** 24 ♘e8+, forking the king and the rook.

**Exercise 4:** 29 ♘e6, forking the queen and rook.

**Exercise 5:** 29...♖e3 and the threat of ...h6-h5 mate is unstoppable.

**Exercise 6:** 29...a4 and Black wins the bishop.

**Exercise 7:** 6 ♘e5 ♕d6 7 c3 (preventing ...♕b4+) 7...♕e6 8 ♕a4 and White wins a piece.

**Exercise 8:** 12 ♗xh7+ ♔h8 13 ♗g6+ ♔g8 14 ♕h7 mate.

**Exercise 9:** 58 ♕a7 any move 59 ♕g1 mate.

**Exercise 10:** 28 ♘e7 mate.

**Exercise 11:** 18 ♖xg7+ ♔xg7 19 ♕g6 ♔h8 20 ♕h7 mate.

**Exercise 12:** 23 ♕xc8 ♖xc8 24 ♖xc8+ with mate to follow.

**Exercise 13:** 30 ♖h6+ ♔g7 31 ♖h7+ ♔xh7 32 ♕xf7+ ♔h8 33 ♘f5 ♖e7 34 ♘xe7 ♖g8 35 ♕xg8 mate.

**Exercise 14:** 33...♕h2+ (any other move and White wins) 34 ♔f3 ♕g3+ (Black now has a variety of ways to win the rook) 35 ♔e4 ♕e3+ 36 ♔f5 ♕xh6.

**Exercise 15:** 24...♘e2+ 25 ♔g2 (25 ♕xe2 loses of course) 25...♕h3+ 26 ♔f3

♗g4 mate.

**Exercise 16:** 22...♗xf4+ 23 exf4 ♖xd4, forking both bishops.

**Exercise 17:** 36...♖xf1+ 37 ♔xf1 ♕d1+ 38 ♕e1 ♘d2+ (38...♗b5+ also mates) 39 ♔g1 ♕xe1 mate.

**Exercise 18:** 14...♘e5 15 ♕b3 ♘xc4 16 ♕xc4 ♘xd5 winning a pawn.

**Exercise 19:** 14...♖xc3 15 bxc3? ♕a3+ 16 ♔d2 ♘e4+, forking the royal pair.

**Exercise 20:** 28 ♖xh7+ ♔xh7 29 ♕xf7+ ♔h6 30 ♖e7 (many other moves win as well) 30...♖h8 31 ♕g7+ ♔h5 32 ♕xh8+ ♔g4 33 ♕h3 mate.

**Exercise 21:** 18...♗a3+ wins the white queen as 19 ♔c2? allows 19...♘d4+ 20 ♔c3 ♕b4 mate.

**Exercise 22:** 46 ♕xc7 ♕xc7 47 ♖b8 ♕b7 48 ♖xb7 ♘xb7 49 ♖b1.

**Exercise 23:** 16...♖d7 17 ♘g5 ♗xd2 18 ♗xd2 ♖xg5.

**Exercise 24:** 10 ♘e5, threatening ♘xc6 and ♕xf7 mate.

**Exercise 25:** 25...♘a1+ 26 ♔c3 ♕xb3+ 27 ♔d2 ♕c2 mate.

**Exercise 26:** 31...b4!.

**Exercise 27:** 22...♗xh2+ 23 ♘xh2 (or 23 ♔h1 ♘xf2 mate) 23...♕xh2 mate.

**Exercise 28:** 23 f6+ Bxf6 24 Qxf6+ Kxf6 25 Bxb6+ Ke7 26 Bxc7.

**Exercise 29:** 25 ♗xe6+ ♔h7 26 ♗f5+ ♔g8 27 ♖c8.

**Exercise 30:** 12...♗xf2+ 13 ♔xf2 ♘g4 + and 14...♘gxe5.

**Exercise 31:** 30 ♖e7 ♗g8 31 ♕a1+ d4 (prevents Black from controlling the a1-h8 diagonal with ...♕b2) 32 ♕f1 c5 33 ♕f4 and the threat of ♕e5+ is unstoppable.

**Exercise 32:** 12...h2+! (many moves win but this is the best) 13 ♔h1 ♕xf2!.

**Exercise 33:** 41 b6!! (amazingly there is no way to stop the pawn) 41...♕e2 42 ♔h3 ♕b2 (there are no more checks after 42. ♕f1+ 43 ♔xh4) 43 b7 and unless Black plays 43...♕xb7 there is no way to stop ♖a8+ followed by b8♕.

**Exercise 34:** 34 ♖h7 (threatening mate with ♖g7) 34...♘h4 (the only move) 35 ♖g7+ ♔h8 36 ♖xg5 ♖e6 37 ♖xh4+ ♖h6 38 ♖xh6 mate.

**Exercise 35:** 41 f6 ♖b5 42 fxg7+ ♕xg7 43 ♕xh5+ ♕h7 44 ♖e8+ ♖xe8 45 ♖xe8+ ♔g7 46 ♖e7+.

**Exercise 36:** 27...♕d1+ 28 ♔f2 ♕xd2+ 29 ♔f3 (29 ♔f1 ♕xd3+ 30 ♔g1 ♕d1+ 31

♔f2 ♕d2+ 32 ♔f1 ♗b5+ 33 ♔g1 ♕e1 mate) 29...♗d1 mate.

**Exercise 37:** 20 ♘e7+ ♗xe7 21 ♖xc8 ♕h3 22 ♖xf8+ ♗xf8 23 ♖d8.

**Exercise 38:** 18...♖xe3+! 19 fxe3 ♗g3+! 20 hxg3 ♕xe3+ and Black will mate.

**Exercise 39:** 21 ♗xe5+!.

**Exercise 40:** 41...♕h2+ 42 ♔f1 ♗f4 43 ♕c3 ♖g6 44 ♕h3 ♕xh3 45 ♗xh3 ♗xd2.

**Exercise 41:** 26 ♕a8 and the rook is lost.

**Exercise 42:** 64 b8♕ ♖xa4+ 65 ♔b3 ♖a3+ 66 ♔xa3.